THE EMERGING TECHNOLOGY READER

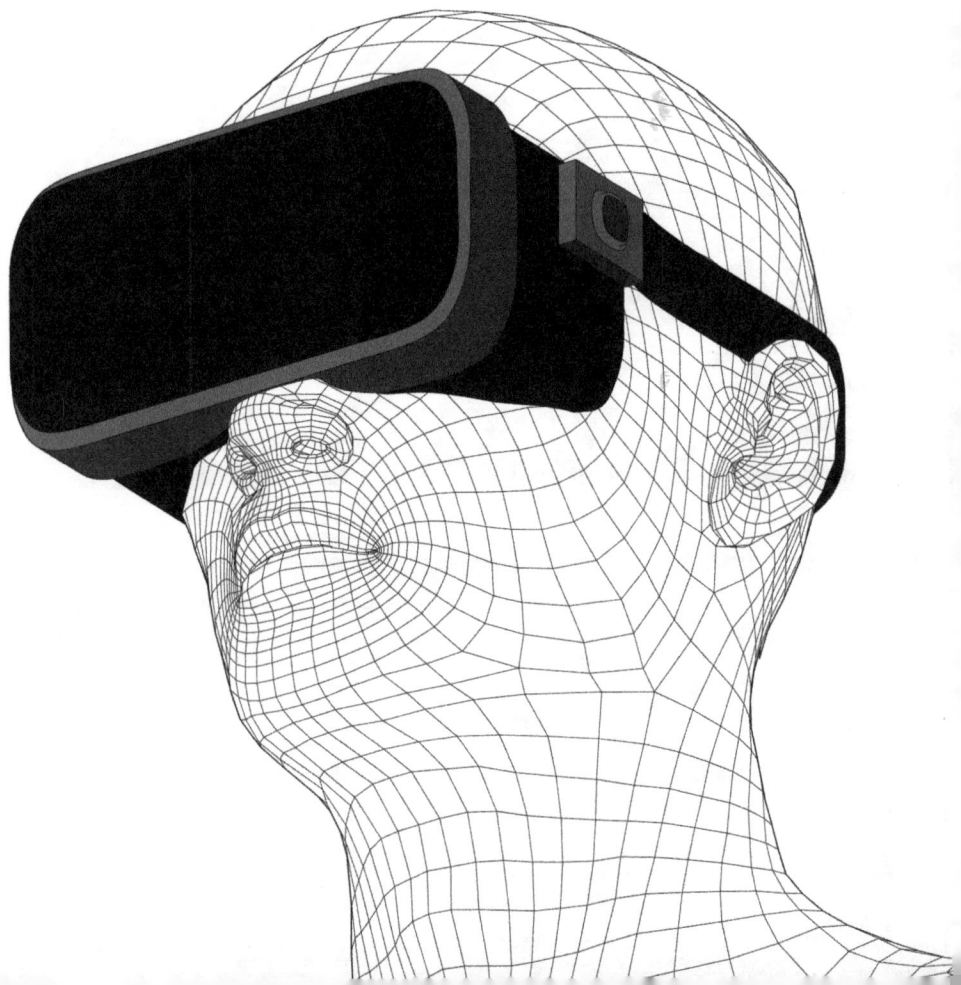

THE EMERGING TECHNOLOGY READER

Edited by Dr. Ray Hsu and Janet Chen

UBC EMERGING MEDIA LAB

2018

UBC EMERGING MEDIA LAB

Published by the Emerging Media Lab, University of British Columbia

Emerging Media Lab
Vancouver Campus
Neville Scarfe Room 1, 2125 Main Mall
Vancouver, BC Canada v6t 1z4
eml.ubc.ca

Edited by Dr. Ray Hsu and Janet Chen

Cover design and typesetting by Carleton Wilson

Acknowledgments

This book was conceptualized, written, and edited at the University of British Columbia and in Vancouver on the traditional, ancestral and unceded territory of the Musqueam, Squamish and Tsleil-Waututh First Nations.

Thank you to the Emerging Media Lab for creating a rare environment for sparking new avenues for knowledge, and to the Department of English for offering the classroom conditions in which to reflect and hone ideas. Thank you to Imogen McIntyre and Carleton Wilson.

Contents

Dr. Ray Hsu 9 Introduction
and Janet Chen

1. EMERGING TECHNOLOGY AND EDUCATION

Ahmed Abdelmoneim 13 Augmented Reality for 3D
Visualization

Caedmon Garayt-Wright 17 Virtual Reality and Multisensory-
Kinesthetic Learning

Benjamin McMaster 21 Classrooms Transitioning into
the New Age of Technology

Brandon Jung 25 Virtual Reality, Hands-On Learning
and Lecture Learning

Jia Yi Zhou 29 Virtual Reality and First-Person Learning

Yi Fan Dai 32 Employable Engineers: Learn to Use VR

Emily Gong 36 VR/AR and English Learning in East Asia

2. EMERGING TECHNOLOGY AND HEALTHCARE

Brooke Cheng 43 Virtual Reality in Stroke Rehabilitation:
Combining the Simulated and Real
Worlds

Anumeet Chepal 49 The Effects and Challenges of Artificial
Intelligence in Medicine

Jennifer Dong   53   Virtual Reality Therapy Incorporating All Psychotherapies

Robert Hebert   57   Reimagining the Harsh Reality of Anxiety in VR

Neriyel Reyes   61   Implementing Virtual Reality into Healthcare Education in order to Decrease Mortality Rates caused by Medical Error

Devon Hayek   66   Augmented Reality and Virtual Reality: Training Surgeons

Matthew Parnian   70   Can Virtual Reality Transfer Laparoscopic Surgical Skills to the Operating Room?

3. EMERGING TECHNOLOGY AND SOCIETY

Kimberly Hsu   77   A New Future for Language: The Internet

Aric Wolstenholme   80   How Can VR Be Used to Improve the Reactions of Ice Hockey Goalies?

Anna (Zhouyu) Yan   84   Developing Virtual Reality Fights Against Gender Inequality In the Video Game Industry

Introduction

Dr. Ray Hsu and Janet Chen

THE WORD TECHNOLOGY borrows from Latin and Greek halves: *techno-* ("form," "art," and related to "craft") and *-logy* (a systematic treatment, related to *logos* as "word" and "discourse"). In the Renaissance, a *technologia* was a treatise on the arts and a systematic treatment of grammar. While this sense seems a far cry from how we have come to understand "technology" in our present day, it also suggests something about the shared roots of the arts and sciences and what opportunities the very idea of technology opens in the classroom.

What is an emerging technology? Building upon its etymological roots, it is a new kind study brought about by new objects of inquiry. It might be said that teachers are tasked with working with students in order to clear a path to these objects. It should be no surprise, then, that proponents of new technologies come to find meaning in their application in educational contexts: that is why there exists the category of "learning technology." What better a context to think through the societal impacts of technology than the classroom, a microcosm of society's future?

It should also be no surprise that healthcare should offer another context in which technology comes to have a meaningful impact on society, for where else could new modes of practice come to be a matter of life and death? At the crux of both healthcare and education lies the university, the institution at which advances in technology open possibilities for research and teaching. From virtual reality to artificial intelligence, from surgeon training to hockey goalie reaction times, the essays in this collection capture the transformational and critical range of these new modes of knowledge and practice.

Just as importantly, the essays in this reader are entirely written by students: those best positioned to notice opportunities for translating knowledge across the different classroom contexts. Why feature writing by students? For two reasons: to close a circle and to showcase the most exciting thought that is coming out of our classrooms. The authors in this collection have each taken an aspect of emerging technology and envisioned futures that they will inherit.

While students have long been tasked with reading the work of distin-guished others, they are almost never entrusted with the power to participate in these dialogues themselves. By seeing the work of their peers in print, we come to have a new kind of peer-review: one that isn't simply an exercise, but one that comes to have stakes in larger conversations that last far beyond the semester.

The authors in this collection are, at heart, researchers on a cutting edge with which they may well be more familiar than the authority figures in the front of the room. They will emerge as voices alongside the technologies that amplify and augment them. Students are perfectly positioned, as the etymol-ogy of *technology* suggests, to work alongside their teachers to find new modes of knowledge prompted by new objects of inquiry.

And that is why this collection matters. It is because the authors have taken a leap into the future: theirs, yours and ours.

1.
EMERGING TECHNOLOGY AND EDUCATION

Augmented Reality for 3D Visualization

Ahmed Abdelmoneim

AUGMENTED REALITY (AR), or mixed reality, has been seeing a surge in popularity and is gaining a lot of interest from many people across different disciplines. The word "Augmented Reality" originates from the verb "augment", which means to make something greater by adding to it. The application of AR is done by taking our own natural environment and adding virtual information on top of it. Although this doesn't sound as interesting as virtual reality, in which a user is completely immersed into a virtual environment, AR can be extremely helpful as it helps introduce a new world in which virtual information can be used to aid everyday activities. Augmented reality software can be developed simply using smartphones or, for more complex applications, using special pieces of hardware like glasses and lenses. Currently, a lot of research is being done about the use of augmented reality in education, as it can be an extremely invaluable technology if used in the right context. This paper will explore how augmented reality can be used to improve 3D visualization of models and concepts taught in courses, with a focus on biology and chemistry. This a problem that many students face when taking these courses. In order to explore an answer to this question, two papers studying the use of augmented reality in chemistry education and molecular biology applications were consulted. The first paper by Chen[1] compares the use of augmented reality and physical models in chemistry education. It focuses on how students interact with AR in comparison to physical models when learning amino acids, and how students perceive AR virtual objects and physical models. The second paper by Gillet et. al[2] explores how models of molecular structures can be created using 3D printing, and how AR can then be integrated with these models. However, before analysing the two papers, we must first understand the strengths in AR technology that helps it provide a solution to this question.

The reason AR can serve as a strong candidate to address this question is it helps capture the attention of students, provides a portable and less expensive alternative to learning materials like physical models, and allows the students to interact with the material in a novel and engaging way. Both papers mention in their introductions how AR provides an intuitive interface for the user. This is because the way a user interacts with virtual objects is very similar to the way they would interact with a similar physical object. This means that a user can "hold" the virtual model, rotate it, and manipulate in the same way they would to a physical model. The significance of this is summarized in a quote in Chen's paper: "Models are the recommended media when realism is essential for learning. Hence, physical models allow students to touch, observe, and to interact with in order to obtain concrete experiences."[1] As humans, we rely on our five senses to explore the world around us, and learning is part of that exploration process. An old Chinese proverb says: "When I hear, I forget. When I see, I remember. When I do, I understand." A lot of the learning done in university courses is based on hearing and seeing, and not much is based on doing, and at the same time, students are expected to fully understand the material. Introducing AR technology into the learning process can provide a way for students to interact with the material component, which adds the doing portion, leading to overall better understanding as a result.

AR has proved itself helpful in adding the doing portion to the learning process, however, is it conceived in the same way as physical models by students? Chen explored an answer to this question in his paper, he conducted a study on four participants who used both AR markers and physical models to observe the structure of amino acids. Chen noted in his discussion that the participants tended to handle the AR model in the same way they did with the physical object. For example, the participants rotated and tilted the AR marker as they did with the physical model, and when counting the number of atoms in the molecule, they counted the number of molecules on the marker and not on the screen. This indicates that AR provides an intuitive way to interact with the structure. In addition, Chen noted in his study that students who liked AR more did so because they thought the physical model was too condensed, while with AR, students were able to zoom in into the model and view it in different ways. This shows the extent of the power AR can have since it can be used to manipulate objects in a way that is not possible for physical models. It is also worth noting that this study was done in 2006, and AR has made huge advancements since then.

In addition to all the advantages AR can add to the educational environment, it can also be integrated with other advancing technologies such as 3D printing. "Augmented reality with Tangible Auto-Fabricated Models for

Molecular Biology Applications" 2 explores how complex 3D models of molecules can be created using 3D printers, and then how they can be augmented using AR. The benefit of this approach is discussed in the introduction of the paper: "Merging physical and virtual objects into an 'augmented reality' (AR) environment enables new modes of interaction through the manipulation of tangible models and the complex information they represent."2 The use of physical models that represent how the actual molecules look like, and integrating that with the benefits of AR mentioned above introduces a new level of realism to the educational process, allowing students to fully visualize the shapes and functions of molecules.

In order to support the benefits of using AR in the classroom, Gillet et al.2 conducted an evaluation of their technology by testing it on high school students. Gillet et al. designed a lesson about basic protein structure concepts, and haemoglobin structure, afterwards, they taught the lesson to high school students and conducted a weeklong technology assessment. "The result suggested that the augmented tangible models were quite engaging and instructive, but we needed to have a more comprehensive lesson plan in order to be most effective."2 This shows that AR along with physical models can, in fact, be used to support the educational process. Another important point is that the cost of the whole process is affordable "Our current approach to tangible computer interfaces for molecular biology has been prototyped in an inexpensive, portable form, using off-the-shelf components."2 In addition to being affordable, using off the shelf component means that providers for this technology don't have to get the equipment from specialized manufacturers, meaning it can be applied easily in many places around the globe, even where technology is not the most advanced.

In conclusion, the use of AR technology in the classrooms to help with visualizing the material has a great potential, as it provides an intuitive and engaging interface, increase learning by doing, can be integrated with other technologies, and is not very expensive. However, as mentioned by Gillet et al.: "We needed to have a more comprehensive plan in order to be most effective."2 Educational techniques must advance in order to be able to cope with the advancement of the technology. However, as part of the digital transformation, the world is going through, AR will be able to integrate itself as one of the main players in this transformation.

Chen, Y. (2006). A study of comparing the use of augmented reality and physical
    models in chemistry education. Proceedings of the 2006 ACM international
    conference on Virtual reality continuum and its applications – VRCIA 06,
    369–372.

Gillet, A., Sanner, M., Stoffler, D., Goodsell, D., & Olson, A. (n.d.). Augmented
    reality with tangible auto-fabricated models for molecular biology applications.
    IEEE Visualization 2004.

Virtual Reality and Multisensory-Kinesthetic Learning

Caedmon Garayt-Wright

VIRTUAL REALITY (VR) is a rapidly advancing field of research in today's society. Older iterations of VR have been used to replace otherwise ineffective or impossible to create scenarios for training purposes. Some of these may include military flight simulations, medical training, and vehicle simulations. These are all great examples of how the pseudo-kinesthetic nature of VR can be used to expedite and improve learning in the industry. Due to VR being an ever-evolving field, the accessibility to the public and levels of immersion that current systems are capable of make VR a promising option for education. Since VR provides an opportunity to experience something in a virtual representation, kinesthetic modes and multisensory of learning can be facilitated. Studies by Laron Shams and Aaron Seitz[1] illustrate how kinesthetic and other multisensory teaching techniques allow people to learn more information, and learn the information quicker than conventional unisensory techniques. Articles by Fällman and Holmlund[2] and Brown and Green[3] highlight the benefits that VR can have on training professionals, as well as advancing education in schools with VR. More related articles by Seo et Al.[4] highlight the promising advancements in VR and how they have been used already. The growth and accessibility of VR may open pathways in education to allow for more abundant multisensory learning, which is shown to improve overall understanding.

Firstly, kinesthetic and multisensory learning is shown to provide an increase in speed and efficiency of learning. Studies show that multisensory learning (learning with material that provokes more than one sense such as a visual and audio presentation) provides much greater benefits in younger children than adults because the developing brain has much higher neural plasticity. Essentially, when the developing brain is introduced to multisensory stimuli, the person is able to retain the information much better and can still remember the topic even when there is only unisensory stimulus; "Bahrick and Lickliter showed that 5-month-old infants could discriminate visually presented rhythms only if they were habituated with auditory-visual presentations of the rhythm and not when habituated with visual-only or auditory-only presentations of rhythm (Shams and Seitz 2008)". In further studies by Shams and Seitz, it was found that even if the stimulus in multisensory learning is incongruent (the information conveyed for each sense is mismatched), the benefits are almost the same as those of unisensory learning, which is indicative of human's ability to match a picture to a sound, even if the two are unrelated. This shows the possible benefits of being able to move away from teaching with PowerPoint slides and revolutionizing education to include more multisensory activities. Virtual reality is a perfect candidate to provide a multisensory environment. For large companies, VR is already a possibility because they have the resources to set up VR simulations, but smaller organizations such as high schools do not possess this buying power. The recent rapid advancements of VR may allow the personal headsets to become an affordable staple in modern education.

Virtual Reality also provides the unique experience of allowing users to manipulate the material that they are presented within 3D space. An example of where this has been useful for students is in a study by Jinsil Hwaryoung Seo et. al. at the Texas A&M University. A program called Anatomy Builder VR was developed that allows users to reconstruct the canine skeletal from the individual bones. The reason for the study is to get a sense of the student's response towards using VR as an education tool, as well as providing an alternative to learning 3D structure with 2D models. Seo et. al. argues that dissection of cadavers may not always be feasible, and "dissection offers only a subtractive and deconstructive perspective (i.e. skin to bone) of the body structure. When students start with the complexity of a complete anatomical specimen, it becomes visually confusing (Seo et Al. 2017)". They also state that "many students have difficulties when mentally visualizing the three dimensional (3D) body from the inside out (i.e. bone to skin), as well as how individual body parts are positioned relative to the entire body (Seo et Al. 2017)", which are both problems that can be solved by Anatomy Builder VR and similar simulations. Due to recent advancements in VR, personal headsets with remote controllers are widely available and for the most part inexpensive. This allows the students to immerse themselves in the simulation and feel as if they are physically piecing the structure together. The construction in 3D space takes away the mental gymnastics of imagining how parts fit together from a 2D picture, as well as providing a greater understanding of how muscles connect to each individual bone, which would eventually become needed knowledge when moving into the professional world.

Furthermore, the current implementations of virtual reality in education have been largely inaccessible to the general public. Expensive machines used for flight simulators provide the extra benefits associated with multisensory learning, but the price tags attached to them cause it to be unfeasible for the everyday person or classroom. The aforementioned headsets provide an immersive learning experience at a price that is much more affordable than previous iterations of VR. The only problem with these currently is that they still may be too pricey for some families or schools to afford. However, there is still a solution. Companies such as Mattel and Google have created devices that are essentially goggles for your smartphone. Google Cardboard and Mattel's View-Master are both products that are either a plastic or cardboard box with two lenses at the end. The desired VR program can be opened on the phone and viewed through the device. It should be understood that this solution provides a much more cost-effective alternative to other VR devices with some viewers being as low as $10 with many free VR programs to choose from. This solution is not without its drawbacks though. Since one would not have the remotes associated with a full VR headset if they choose a smartphone viewer, they would not be able to get the kinesthetic aspect of learning. This budget conscious solution still provides users with the immersion in 3D space, and may also come with audio stimulation depending on the software. A pure price reduction is not the only thing that can cause an abundance of VR. A cultural shift may also be happening in the modern world which would allow VR headsets to become commonplace in the household. In recent years, VR has gained a lot of traction in the public; many more people are aware of its existence and have tried or owned a headset. The openness to VR and it's staggering reductions in price may allow it to become as common as a cell phone in today's society.

Overall, recent hardware and software advances in virtual reality are making it possible to create an environment that fosters multisensory and kinesthetic learning. There are apparent benefits of multisensory learning, but the drawback is that it is harder to implement; especially with the budgets of public schools. If VR grows as an industry it will be much easier to implement in less funded areas of education, and it will also be much easier to create programs that are specific to a class' learning needs.

Shams, Ladan, and Aaron R. Seitz. "Benefits of multisensory learning." *Trends in cognitive sciences* 12.11 (2008): 411–417.

Fällman, Daniel, Anders Backman, and Kenneth Holmlund. "VR in education: An introduction to multisensory constructivist learning environments." *Conference on University Pedagogy (Umea University, Umea, Sweden, February 18–19)*. 1999.

Brown, Abbie, and Tim Green. "Virtual reality: Low-cost tools and resources for the classroom." *TechTrends* 60.5 (2016): 517–519.

Seo, Jinsil Hwaryoung, et al. "Anatomy Builder VR: Embodied VR Anatomy Learning Program to Promote Constructionist Learning." *Proceedings of the 2017 CHI Conference Extended Abstracts on Human Factors in Computing Systems*. ACM, 2017.

Classrooms Transitioning into the New Age of Technology

Benjamin McMaster

THE TRADITIONAL ANIMAL dissection is a key part of an education in biology and has been a common learning tool for decades across western civilization classrooms (Lalley et al., 2009). The procedure provides a hands-on learning experience for students, providing them with a physical understanding of the anatomy of a species. However, as much as a dissection is educational, there are many problems associated with the practice. For example, according to PETA "there are very real moral and ethical concerns over killing an animal for the sake of learning (Lalley et al.,189)." As well the decay of specimen's compromises results and due to high costs students must share the specimens (Lalley et al.). However, as developed countries transition into a new era of technologies and virtual worlds, so should the world of education. More specifically, virtual reality technologies can be used in lieu of traditional physical dissection methods, mitigating these disadvantages of using deceased animals. Virtual reality can be viewed as any technology where a virtual model is being created on an electronic device, ranging from models developed in computer programs, all the way to fully immersive technologies that use sensors and goggles to transport the user into a technologically manufactured world. In a classroom setting, virtual reality can be used as a learning tool to replace dissections and further a student's understanding of the material. Also, at higher levels of education, these technologies can still be applied when medical school students are taught proper surgical procedures. Nevertheless, there are still factors that prevent these technologies from being adopted as a complete replacement of dissections. As the use of technologies in everyday life becomes universal, the use of virtual reality as a learning tool for dissections and surgical procedures will be able to revolutionize education and transition the traditional classroom into this new age of technology.

Virtual reality programs and technologies have the potential to replace physical dissection in the traditional classroom setting and better educate students on the anatomy of a specimen. To do this, virtual reality technologies use programs that mimic physical dissections, using computers and simulators rather than a deceased animal. Lalley et al. explain how a program called V-Frog, developed by "Tactus Technologies," uses 3D virtual reality technology to replace the use of frogs dissected in the classroom. The replacement of animals contributes to a more ethically sound classroom were no dilemmas exist because of animals needing to give their lives for education. Furthermore, emerging technologies, such as virtual reality, provide students with an ameliorated understanding of anatomy compared to students performing a traditional dissection. An experiment performed by Lalley et al. concluded that "students completing virtual dissections had higher learning (posttest) scores, indicating that they learned more than those completing physical dissections (Lalley et al., 196)." This higher achievement by students performing a virtual dissection clearly means virtual reality is more than a viable option to replace traditional dissection. Also, when the students in Lalley et al's experiment were given a test to analyze their retention of the material covered during both physical and virtual dissection, both students scored similarly. This further indicates that the use of technology can more than adequately replace physical dissections. Finally, Lalley et al. report that participation of students in the experiments is much greater with virtual reality methods. This increase in participation is due to the fact that students who would be otherwise uncomfortable with performing the dissection have no issues with the virtual simulator. As a result of higher participation, more students are gaining knowledge with the material leading virtual reality to become a more effective learning tool. Not only do these new learning tools based on virtual reality overcome the shortcomings of a traditional dissection, they also further develop students' education.

Similar to dissections in the classroom, the use of virtual reality has been shown in a study performed by Ahlberg et al., to reduce the error rates of resident medical students as they start transitioning into medical procedures from the classroom and mock settings. These benefits of emerging technologies are crucial, since, unlike a classroom dissection, medical procedures take place with high stakes and a person's life in the future medical-professionals hands. To commence, the study explains how virtual reality is used to mimic complex procedures such as laparoscopies, an abdominal surgical procedure, to help prepare the students (Ahlberg et al., 797). The technology is used to help students gain a deeper understanding of the procedure in a low-risk environment. Furthermore, the study explains the how "a clear learning curve in laparoscopic surgery has been described as the period before acceptable technical proficiency is reached, during which time the risk for complications clearly is increased (Ahlberg et al., 197)." An obvious need for virtual reality as a learning tool is apparent from the findings of the experiment. Using a virtual reality program called "LapSim," the students gained valuable low-risk experience regarding the procedure and were able to achieve much greater success when it came to performing the procedure. Ahlberg et Al's experiment outlined the usefulness and success of modern technologies, such as virtual reality, in high-level education systems.

Contrarily, as with many developing technologies and learning tools, there exist negatives results of using virtual reality devices in lieu of performing physical dissections. Firstly, although there are many studies such as the one performed by Lalley et al. and Ahlberg et al., with conclusions indicating that students have better performance on examination when they use virtual reality methods, there are still some studies that claim the opposite. For example, Lalley et al. discuss how "in some cases there were no differences in learning found between physical and virtual dissection (Lalley et al., 190)" and that "Marszalek & Lockard (1999) found that adolescent science students completing a physical dissection produced superior learning gains from pretest to posttest when compared to Digital Frog®, a multimedia dissection application (Lalley et al. 190)." The contradicting outcomes of these different experiments illustrate a need for further research into the advantages of virtual reality to form a definitive conclusion on whether the students' grasp of the material is ameliorated by using these technologies. Furthermore, all studies conclude that over time, the differences in retention of material by the students dissipate. When students are examined after a certain time period later on the material covered in a dissection, the scores of the students who performed the dissection physically and those who performed a virtual dissection are roughly equal and lower than the original post-dissection tests (Lalley et al., 196). It becomes evident then, that virtual reality technologies are not improving the long-term memory of students in the classroom, reducing the benefits of said technologies. Finally, a common concern that educators have about switching from physical dissection methods to virtual dissection methods is that the virtual technologies will be unable to replace the curiosity and fascination aspects that traditional dissections provide. As advanced as the current state of virtual reality technologies is, it is still not possible to mimic the exactly the same emotions that individuals feel during a real-life dissection. However, as the state of technology develops at an astronomical rate, the experience virtual reality provides is becoming closer and closer to fully replacing physical dissections. As numerous as the benefits of virtual reality and other technologies similar are, there are still drawbacks that create hesitance for educators at all levels to adopt them.

The use of virtual reality programs and technologies in all levels of education demonstrates the ability to change the education for better, specifically as a learning tool to replace traditional dissections. Although these new technologies bring with them negative aspects, the use of virtual reality has the potential to improve traditional educational tools such as dissections. New technologies can reduce the negative aspects of physical dissections such as mitigating the moral and ethical dilemmas that dissections create, the decay of specimens and the aversion of some students to participate. As well, the use of these technologies better educates students in varying levels of education, ranging from secondary school to high-level medical school. It is evident that the future of education lies in the transition of traditional classrooms into the modern world of technology.

WORKS CITED

Ahlberg, Gunnar, et al. "Proficiency-Based Virtual Reality Training Significantly Reduces the Error Rate for Residents during Their First 10 Laparoscopic Cholecystectomies." *The American Journal of Surgery*, vol. 193, no. 6, 2007, pp. 797–804., doi: 10.1016/j.amjsurg.2006.06.050.

Lalley, James P, et al. "A Comparison of V-Frog© to Physical Frog Dissection." *International Journal of Environmental and Science Education*, vol. 5, no. 2, ser. 189–200, Apr. 2010. 189–200.

Virtual Reality, Hands-On Learning and Lecture Learning

Brandon Jung

A COMMON CHALLENGE in modern-day education for teachers is to find the optimal way of teaching their students. The fact that everybody learns differently presents the difficulty of making their teaching method suitable for all students. Some students are hands-on learners and others learn best from lectures. Having virtual or augmented reality would pose a solution to this problem by providing a more versatile method of teaching that allows the teacher to create an optimal teaching method for each student (Byrne, 2). Each student would have their own unique learning experience that is tailored to how they learn best, improving both the productivity of teaching time and the knowledge gained by the students (Allison, 1).

Hands-on learners learn the best when they are taught by experimenting with tangibles. With the use of virtual or augmented reality, hands-on learners would be able to experience telepresence, which, ideally, means that they feel as though what they see in their virtual world is real. Virtual reality would allow the possibilities of experimenting to be virtually limitless, such as being able to conduct experiments on the moon to test the effects of gravity or experimenting with chemical reactions safely (Allison, 160). Many classes use websites with simulations that show students the effects of changing variables in a system, similarly, with virtual reality, students can observe up-close what happens when they change settings in their world.

The education system in today's society often supports lectures with labs to solidify the material being taught. However, many possible lab ideas are limited by the practicality of bringing in equipment, as well as the safety and cost of using certain material. With the use of virtual reality, expensive and large equipment could be used by students in a virtual world without schools having to pay for the equipment or the possibility of the equipment being broken. For example, bringing in or building a low gravity chamber would take a lot of work to build, in addition to being very expensive. Virtual reality would allow students to make use of such equipment that they would otherwise not have access to. Also, certain science experiments are not able to be done due to jeopardizing the safety of students. Many science experiments, such as chemical explosions and examining dangerous viruses, could be conducted in a virtual world because of the lack of threat to the safety of those doing the experiment. Reducing the limitations of what experiments could be done safely in a lab, teachers, and schools would be able to provide students an option of learning that is more hands-on and lab-oriented as opposed to classes mainly composed of lectures.

Virtual reality is not only limited to helping those who are hands-on learners but will also provide a more optimal method of teaching to those who learn best from lectures. Through improving the demonstrations done in class by the teacher, the efficiency of how well the material is taught also increases. If a lecture was being done inside of a virtual world, instead of powerpoint slides, teachers or students could make a simulation of the material being taught. By allowing students to create a part or the whole virtual world based on a topic they're learning, they would exercise their understanding of the topic to the teacher while simultaneously staying engaged due to enjoying their work (Byrne, 5). Instead of having students imagine how the shape of a molecule would look like using balloons, a life-size molecule could appear in front of them, with the ability to be manipulated and changed based on what is being taught or observed (Byrne, 1). In addition, if you were learning about how a molecule reacts with other molecules, virtual reality would allow you to observe how they interact, if they form bonds, and what the bonds look like. Often times, small details are omitted by a teacher when teaching because it may cause confusion to students as they try to follow the teacher's train of thought. However, by showing a demonstration in a virtual world, students would be able to see the material and make conclusions on their own (Byrne, 4). Similar to what was stated before, virtual reality would allow teachers to have a wider range of possible demonstrations in class, due to the reduction in limitations in practicality. Allowing a teacher to provide better examples during lectures would not only increase the effectiveness of what they are trying to explain but also gives students a more interactive lecture which would increase the efficiency of each lecture.

As mentioned before, the education system in today's society is very lecture-oriented, making it difficult for those who are hands-on learners to efficiently learn. Virtual reality poses a possible solution to this by allowing labs to be more versatile, thus making it more practical to teach more topics. School's today are often limited to small experiments using cheap equipment that is sufficient in providing a basic understanding of the material being taught. With the use of virtual reality, labs can be used to teach how atoms are arranged in solids, liquids, and gases, the effects of moving at near light speed, and other experiments that would otherwise be impossible to experience in real life. Although telepresence isn't fully optimized to provide an ideal experience, with the virtual reality technology we have today, students can still learn from doing labs in a virtual world.

By being able to do virtually any experiment on a given topic, a discussion about separating labs and lectures in university to be its own class would be possible. Right now, labs are not sufficient in teaching all the material in a course because of the limitations of what we can do experiments on. As well, lectures are not able to provide a demonstration in which you can observe closely what happens as certain variables are changing. Labs are often designed to solidify material learned in previous lectures but are rarely used as a learning opportunity. As a result, those who are struggling or not caught up in their lectures will not benefit as much in their labs because the labs are designed assuming you know the basic concepts. By separating labs and lectures, labs can be redesigned to be a learning experience, where students learn by discovery and obtain knowledge by fabricating conclusions based on their observations. With the use of virtual reality, students would be able to create their own virtual world in which they can explore on their own. The benefit of allowing students to create their own world is a sense of accomplishment and pride that comes with finishing their world (Byrne, 8). Being able to experience and see what they made themselves would encourage them to expand on their work, which in turn generates more of an interest in the work they're doing (Allison, 2).

Often times teachers creating lesson plans are limited in options because of practicality and attempting to provide the perfect balance to provide an optimal learning experience for every student. With the use of virtual reality, the separation of labs and lectures would grant both hands-on learners and lecture learners a more efficient learning environment. This would allow teachers to predict the learning method of their students based on if it was a lab or lecture, and create a lesson plan that is best suited to that learning method.

WORKS CITED

Allison, Don, and Larry F. Hodges. "Virtual Reality for Education?" *Proceedings of the ACM Symposium on Virtual Reality Software and Technology – VRST '00*, 2000, doi:10.1145/502390.502420.

Byrne, C. (1993). Virtual reality and education. Proceedings of IFIP WG3.5 International Workshop Conference, pp. 181–189

Virtual Reality and First-Person Learning

Jia Yi Zhou

IN MOST SCIENCE CLASSES, thinking in three dimensions is required to further develop the student's understanding of theories and concepts. The learning environment provided by the current education system has a limitation to the extent that knowledge which requires the thinking in three dimensions is difficult to construct. The knowledge constructed by learning out of context, which is a pedagogical method that predominates at school, is deficient because it is not as relevant as a learning by directly interacting with the content (Curcio, Dipace & Norlund, 2016, p. 64). A study performed by Winn (1993) suggests that virtual reality allows students to be immersed in the virtual environment and interact with it (para.3). In light of Winn's study, the application of virtual reality in education can help students overcome the limitation in the current education system in which the learning environment is insufficient for learning that requires three-dimensional thinking.

Three-dimensional thinking defined as "the thinking required to determine the position of an object," presents a unique learning challenge for students (Curcio et. al, 2016, p. 64). In particular, the cell biology course that I am currently taking often requires thinking in three dimensions. In cellular processes such as protein synthesis, the learning requires me to visualize the size, distance, and position of DNA and RNA molecules and how they interact in the cell. Taking note of Winn's study, virtual reality is able to "place participants in environments that provided them with just the information they needed and with which they could interact as naturally as they could with the real world" (1993, para. 3). Immersion in a virtual cell would allow me to manipulate the relative size, distance, and position of molecules and learn in the process of interactions. As a result, my learning is boosted by the improvement of my ability to think in three dimensions, which motivates me to learn by directly interacting with the molecules. Therefore, virtual reality can create learning environments that cannot be created using traditional strategies and this quality makes it superior to other kinds of pedagogical method.

Virtual reality provides students with situated learning that is more relevant and successful than learning out of context. Introduced by Winn (1993), virtual reality simulates the real world, which allows students to learn while they are "situated in the context" such that their learning can be applied (para. 13). Virtual reality allows students to move away from simply 'learning' a subject or topic to 'feeling' the content. For example, virtual reality can be applied to my cell biology class. As described in my biology textbook, purine bases pair with pyrimidine bases because they have the same geometry that stabilizes the DNA molecule (Morris, Hartl, Knoll, & Lue, 2016, pp. 40). My knowledge about DNA structure obtained from the textbook is deficient because it is not as relevant as a direct interaction with a DNA model. However, the virtual environment allows me to be immersed in a cell and directly interact with a DNA molecule. By changing the base pairs and watching the effects of the wrong base pairs have on the stability of the DNA structure, my knowledge about DNA structure would be strengthened. Therefore, this immersive technology is equally important as learning out of context because it enhances our learning with personal, subjective, and direct experiences with course contents.

Virtual reality is capable of providing students with a first-person learning experience that cannot be obtained in formal education (Curcio et. al, 2016, p. 62). Informal education, students are familiar with third-person learning, such as learning theories and concepts out of textbooks. For instance, the materials in my cell biology class is challenging because learning protein synthesis from the textbook is insufficient for me to visualize and understand the directionality and assembly of DNA and RNA molecules. In contrast to first-person learning, third-person learning is objective and indirect because the textbook is a description of knowledge constructed by someone else. As suggested by Winn, "first-person experiences account for a great deal of individuals' activity in the world and their learning about it" (1993, para. 12). In light of Winn's idea, virtual reality is a great tool that can assist me to overcome the challenge presented in my cell biology class. It is able to provide me with a first-person learning experience that is not available in a classroom, such as directly interacting with DNA and RNA molecules and watching their assembly as if I am inside a cell. Therefore, virtual reality allows us to create from our experiences the kind of knowledge that is only accessible through direct real-life experiences, never through any of the third-person experiences that predominate in school. Hence, virtual reality promotes the best strategy that allows students to learn from first-person experience.

With some exceptions, educators have not made the connection between classroom learning and virtual reality, thereby they miss the opportunity to provide students with a more involved pedagogical method. Schools should pay attention to the birth of virtual reality and plan effectively before incorporating it into curriculum. The learning challenge created by the requirement of three-dimensional thinking in some classes can be solved by the use of virtual reality. The immersion in a virtual environment provides students with situated learning which is more relevant than learning out of content. It assists students to overcome the limitation of third-person learning experience provided by the current education system. The direct involvement with course materials enhances students' learning and strengthens their ability to apply theories and concepts. Therefore, the application of virtual reality in education can assist students to improve their ability to think in three dimensions, increase their interactions with course materials, and help to gain first-person learning experience.

WORKS CITED

Curcio, I. D., Dipace, A., & Norlund, A. (2016). Virtual realities and education. *Research on Education and Media, 8*(2), 60–68.

Winn, W. (1993). A conceptual basis for educational applications of virtual reality. *Technical Publication R-93-9, Human Interface Technology Laboratory of the Washington Technology Center.* Seattle: University of Washington.

Morris, J., Hartl, D. L., Knoll, A. H., & Lue, R. (2016). The molecules of life. *Biology: How life works* (pp. 39–45). New York, NY: W.H. Freeman & Company, a Macmillan Education Imprint.

Employable Engineers: Learn to Use VR

Yi Fan Dai

IN THE WORLD of engineering, industry problems are usually complex and conveyed through descriptions via numerous project documents (Abulrub et al., 751). To prepare engineering graduates for the workplace, academic institutions oftentimes include adequate amounts of laboratory time into the timetables for students to gain real-life design experience; an opportunity to train in independent thinking and demonstrate reporting technical information (751). This paper aims to discover the effects of virtual technology integration in 3D modeling and its effects on engineering students.

In an industry driven by deadlines, integration of virtual reality technology in the workplace has been proven to be a cost and time-efficient solution to maximizing the engineering design cycle (751). With progressive implementations of virtual reality into engineering education, students are able to map out the problems with higher clarity and create more precise solutions through hyper-realistic aids and immersive visualizations (Messner et al.).

Such claims were tested by researchers from Pennsylvania State University and The University of Warwick. Both projects showcase the profitability of VR through examining the construction process by their undergraduates in their respective sectors of infrastructure (Messner et al., 2003) and automobile design (Abulrub et al., 2010).

In comparison to the past where models were drawn with 3D Computer-aided Design software (CAD) and viewed through flat computer screens, VR allows for the imitations of real-life materials and extreme details of proposed designs. Currently, while new undergraduates are coming into universities with higher fluency in computer use and innovative software, the workforce is also moving forwards in real-time with more implementations of digital planning much earlier in their design process than previously been done (Messner et al.). To keep up with changing times, academic institutions must adapt to and adopt these technological advancements to ensure their graduates are prepared for a successful transition into the workforce (Messner et al.).

In the 2003 publication by Messner et al., "Using Virtual Reality to Improve Construction engineering Education" the authors present their research of VR and "4D CAD modeling (3D design plus time)" implementations in their undergraduate Architectural Engineering program (Messner et al.). As construction cost estimate and planning is often a key part of an engineer's role, currently the students learn to analyze design plans and construction sequences from 2D images, outlining complicated schedules of their building projects.

The research was done with a group of 25 fifth-year undergraduates. The students were tested to see if they were able to better interpret and identify potential schedule errors through a review of Critical Path Method (CPM) schedule compared to an analysis done by using a 4D CAD model. Two major schedule conflicts were intentionally placed into the design plan and students were asked to review said plan for constructability with the objective being whether they were able to correctly identify the two issues. Then the same students created the 4D CAD model of the same building model and were then asked to complete the same review for building sequence. Out of the 25 students, when analyzing with the more traditional method of CPM, 52% identified issue 1, consisted of safety issue in assembling concrete slab and steel column, while only 28% discovered issue 2, a physical construction sequence error in installing the windows of the third floor (Messner et al.). The numbers raised drastically when compared with the results than that of the 4D CAD, 84% of the students recognized issue 1, and a near-perfect score of 92% (23 out of 25) of the students realizing the error with installing windows (Messner et al.). This heightened ability to visualize solutions enables students to practice real-time technical demands from the industry but as well as improved their ability to review constructability of building projects and construction plans for complex buildings and infrastructure. With the visualization aids such as VR, the students can be projected to produce fewer errors in their work which ultimately translates to more effective engineering design plans, cutting down in time and costs of any project (Messner et al.).

Similarly in Abulrub et al.'s 2010 publication of "Virtual Reality in Engineering Education: the Future of Creative Learning," the authors emphasizes the necessity of implementing VR systems in the current education system to producing engineering students to meet industry demands. The Warwick Project was designed to highlight the effective role VR has in their NPI (New Product Introduction) process. The Warwick University Formula Student Design Team students were trained in using virtual reality in their design process in preparation for the Formula Competition. The primary task was for the team to analyze their design concept in collaboration with one another with 3D glasses.

In this case, the automotive industry was used as an example in demonstrating the potential difficulty in bridging engineering students with the workplace. Highly driven by aesthetics, the automotive industry now not only focuses on producing highly functional cars, but must go above-and-beyond for their customers with both luxurious appearances and user comfort. In addition to their technical skills, engineering students must have mastery over a wider variety of skills from for their clients (Abulrub et al., 757). The Warwick Design Team mentioned numerous times the importance of aesthetics in their design. By providing their clients with compelling visual details and hyper-realistic actualization of their proposed design, the team was able to secure enough sponsors to fund their design (756). This imitates real-world scenarios where the engineers are not only technically equipped but must have proficiency in marketing their own ideas as well. Not only so, during the team review of the car, the team was able of finding 88 additional concerns that were identified virtually with their VR headsets(754). Small "gaps and seethroughs" were recognized in their assessment of the CAD model, all of which were eventually resolved before the team committed to a physical prototype (754). The team included in their final conclusion of the benefits that VR technology, specifically aiding them to catch the small errors that might have otherwise been overlooked with traditional methods (754).

It is recognized that engineered solutions must possess good design, which embodies both superb visuals and extreme functionality, and with that follows the necessity to equip future engineers with the required skillset in virtual systems to expand their solutions to the fullest extent technologically possible (757). By allowing engineering students the flexibility to change their solutions, numerous designs can be simultaneously explored to sufficient amounts before any definite decision-making (757). VR can provide more in-depth comprehension and application of different design options within the same timeframe than that of using traditional methods (Messner et al.).

Through the implementations of VR in design labs, engineering students are able to expand the boundaries of their creative work to producing "unique, realistic and practical solutions (Amman et al.,756)," all while gaining a higher understanding in their technical fields, enabling them to successfully align with industry standards before the end of their university careers. By doing as such, graduates are ultimately producing innovative work all while saving production costs and time for their prospective employers. While the cost of expanding educational equipment, with respect to both time and finances, may be a debate for some (Messner et al.), the authors hope that by highlighting examples of increased productivity with VR implementations in academia, more schools will realize that by supporting the development of VR technology, they are also investing in the future of their students as well.

WORKS CITED

Abulrub, Abdul-Hadi G., et al. "Virtual Reality in Engineering Education: The Future of Creative Learning ." *Learning Environments and Ecosystems in Engineering Education* , 4 Apr. 2010, pp. 751–757. *IEEE Global Engineering Education Conference (EDUCON)*

Messner, John I., et al. "Using Virtual Reality to Improve Construction Engineering Education." *American Society of Engineering Education, 2003. American Society of Engineering Education Annual Conference and Exposition.*

VR/AR and English Learning in East Asia

Emily Gong

IN MANY EAST Asian countries, English, being a universal language, is a mandatory subject, for it is essential for professional communication and development. However, learning English is often tedious and difficult, especially in a non-English environment. Moreover, students would only learn the basics, such as grammar, but not the Western culture. Consequently, this is a waste of the students' time and educational resources. Meanwhile, as I reflect on my personal experience with English learning in East Asian schools, I notice that the methods were not innovative, so it became my particular interest to find ways for current high school students in Asia to gain an improved learning experience. At the present time, two promising candidates for improving learning experience are virtual reality (VR) and augmented reality (AR): the former immerses users in a computer-simulated environment, and the latter is the integration of artificial images and information with real-world surroundings. As these two technologies gain their popularity in the scientific world, people are investigating their usefulness for educational purposes. In fact, this new way of learning and teaching is currently being studied and experimented in Western schools and making its way to East Asian schools. This paper argues that VR and AR can help students to gain interest in learning English in the context of East Asian schools.

To begin with, AR can help students to be engaged in learning challenging concepts by involving the students in an interactive learning environment. In a case study done in Taiwan, students went around campus and pointed their mobile phones to their surroundings (Liu & Tsai, 2012). Then, the device would calculate the students' positions with a GPS system and produce a virtual scene with labels around objects. The students could then click on these objects and view the object's detailed description in English. After this learning process, the students were asked to compose a descriptive essay. By analysing their writings, researchers found that the students generally incorporated the materials learnt through AR into their own writing, and some even related this knowledge with their own experiences. In other words, AR learning helped students to gain a deeper understanding of the definitions in textbooks by connecting those materials learnt in a classroom setting with a visual object. Not only did AR provided linguistic knowledge for the students, it helped them write essays that are not generic, but rather meaningful to them. Most importantly, students found this process more enjoyable and engaging than sitting in a classroom as they mentioned in their essays. Notably, they were able to learn more effectively and efficiently by immersing themselves in their process of learning English, and this encourages them to develop an interest.

Moreover, VR encourages students to communicate actively in English; thus, it improves their speaking skills while increasing their confidence levels. When students learn English through VR, they are usually represented by an avatar in a 3D virtual world (VW) setting, and many interactive functions are available, including a chat tool that allows them to communicate with other users. In a review paper analysing the research done on VW in an educational setting, the author concluded 3 important usages: Communication Spaces, Simulation of Spaces, and Experimental Spaces (Hew & Cheung, 2010). First, the communication space allows users to share ideas verbally and non-verbally, such as through emotions and actions of the avatar. As learners hold a conversation in English, the language's syntax and vocabulary are reinforced. Also, with constant practice, learners usually become more confident with communicating in English. Next, the simulation of space allows users to be immersed in a 3D learning environment. For instance, this 3D characteristic of VR was especially important in university virtual campus tours, assisting International students to familiarize with the campus before actually arriving at the respective university. Similar to campus tours, simulation in educational settings can help students understand a challenging concept. As an illustration, many idioms in the English language are awkward to translate, and this problem is easily solved with visualizing the idioms in a virtual situation, where the learner directly perceive how these concepts are used in the daily life of a native English speaker. Lastly, the experiential spaces imply that "acting" in VW or controlling the avatar in VR settings help with the student's learning since they were able to put themselves in the situation of the virtual figure and reflect critically on the English learnt through this program. The three key uses of VW, which are communication spaces, simulation of paces, and experimental spaces, help to develop a student's speaking skills and to promote confidence in English communication.

Most importantly, VR and AR might help East Asian students take learning into their own hands and gain more interest. Unlike how Western education is student-centered, (meaning that the focus is on the individual learner and collaboration and mutual communication with the teacher are encouraged,) education in East Asia is teacher-centered, where the focus is on the teacher, and students listen for the instructions from the teacher. (Hew & Cheung, 2010). In fact, most Asian students are pressured by their parents, their teachers, and the society to study rigorously and follow a career path that has already been laid out for them. Students often find themselves learning for the sake of satisfying the society's standards and not for themselves. Conversely, VR and AR gives students control over their learning and builds their confidence in learning a new material like a foreign language. In a Western study done on VW in education, a student reported that "[VW] allows [students] to learn at [their] own pace guided by [their] own interests" (Bronack, Riedl, & Tashner, 2006). Students were able to learn independently, a feature that is absent in Asian learning environments. To add on, VR learning offers the liberty for the students to pursue their own learning preferences, and this freedom allows students to truly enjoy the beauty of learning since they can decide for themselves the most appealing and productive way for them to learn a foreign language. From the positive feedback of many VR experiments, we can see the possibility for VR and AR to transform a compulsory yet boring English learning process into a pleasing one.

Nonetheless, VR and AR face a critical problem in the practical application that can be solved with the actual implementation of VR/AR devices. To start, in these VR experiments, fast-typing skills and spontaneous reaction were necessary for the conversation to proceed, as the chat function was the primary way of communicating with one another (Hew & Cheung, 2010). Additionally, in the study mentioned earlier, where the students used AR to learn about the different objects around campus in English, one participant did not use the mobile device at all since he was unfamiliar with using this technology. These two examples bring awareness to the fact that not every student is comfortable or compatible with technology, especially in rural parts of Eastern Asia, where students often do not receive the opportunity to learn about information technology before university. Many people in rural areas disagree with technology education and prefer traditional learning in a classroom. However, this problem will dissipate once VR and AR are introduced into a real classroom setting and the significance of computer-related education is realized. These problems remain a limitation to experimenting VR and AR in education.

In conclusion, VR and AR have the potential to help East Asian students learn English in an enjoyable way. VR and AR assist students in learning difficult concepts by visualizing the problem and involving the students in their learning while encompassing their own culture. Currently, more studies are taking place in Eastern Asia and hopefully, they will soon find their applications in a real classroom setting.

WORKS CITED

Hew, K. F., & Cheung, W. S. (2010). Use of three-dimensional (3-D) immersive virtual worlds in K-12 and higher education settings: A review of the research. *British Journal of Educational Technology, 41*(1), 33–55. doi:10.1111/j.1467-8535.2008.00900.x

Liu, P.-H. E. and Tsai, M.-K. (2013), Using augmented-reality-based mobile learning material in EFL English composition: An exploratory case study. *British Journal of Educational Technology,* 44: E1–E4. doi:10.1111/j.1467-8535.2012.01302.x

Stephen Bronack, Richard Riedl & John Tashner (2006) Learning in the zone: A social constructivist framework for distance education in a 3-dimensional virtual world, Interactive Learning Environments, 14:3, 219-232, DOI: 10.1080/10494820600909157

2.
EMERGING TECHNOLOGY
AND HEALTHCARE

Virtual Reality in Stroke Rehabilitation: Combining the Simulated and Real Worlds

Brooke Cheng

AS THE WORLD population steadily ages, devastating conditions such as strokes are becoming increasingly prevalent.[1] Current, traditional rehabilitation techniques (physiotherapy and occupational therapy) for this condition have proven to be effective to an extent, but newfound technology is creating opportunities for growth in the healthcare system. Virtual Reality (VR), for example, encapsulates the use of three-dimensional gaming simulations of real scenarios which can be applied to the entertainment, educational and health industries.[2] A pattern of an existing deficit in the effectiveness of traditional therapy has formed across the current contours of stroke rehabilitation. VR, a multifaceted and modern method of rehabilitation, is breaking new ground outside of this recurring observation. Many barriers, largely related to limited research and a restricted target audience, lie in the way of achieving the implementation of VR technology as a common method of stroke rehabilitation. However, this paper argues that VR technology should be further adopted in health care for stroke rehabilitation as it improves upon current traditional therapy through both practical elements (locational flexibility and transportability) and emotional dimensions (motivation and personal engagement).

Virtual Reality (VR) is a "computer-based technology that allows users to interact with a multisensory simulated environment".[2] It controls the information received by sensory organs to create a virtual scene which feels like reality.[3] This new technology can range from non-immersive equipment (video game systems) to fully immersive environments (ranging from entry-level VR hardware such as the Google Cardboard to the most sophisticated Oculus Rift headsets).[2] With the most complex technology, users feel fully isolated from their surroundings.[2] Among several possible applications, VR use has been shown to be effective in the field of *neuroplasticity*, the repetitive and task-oriented training of the brain.[2]

Strokes affect a process known as the mirror-neuron system, where the normal adult brain fires neurons at a growing rate when observing motion.

However, the injured neurological systems of stroke victims must have this system rewired to induce reorganization and recovery of the brain. VR enables patients to interact in a three-dimensional virtual world and to simultaneously observe avatar movements on screens. It reactivates the mirror-neuron system of the brain through computer-generated simulations.[4]

In this way, VR allows the outside world to be brought to the patient while they are unable to access it themselves. As a result of lost neurological blood flow, both motor and balance skills can become impaired due to stroke; this loss of mobility makes motion difficult within the clinic, let alone busy public areas. Most traditional rehabilitation methods require the labour of healthcare workers and transportation to specialized facilities outside a hospital, which can be "tedious, resource-intensive and costly".[4] For stroke patients who suffer from mobility impairment or lack access to treatment facilities, such a procedure may not be feasible. Due to this setback, the need for alternative stroke rehabilitation methods has increased. The gaming systems of VR have developed formats that are applicable to home use, increasing the levels of affordability and comfort associated with rehabilitation.[4] VR games "can be performed safely and effectively at any time and at any location including within and outside rehabilitation sessions with older adults, those with mild Alzheimer's disease, and [those] over 70 years of age".[1] Recovery performed at home, especially for elderly victims, prevents the disillusionment of the patient from their previous lifestyle and smoothly reintegrates them back into social interaction. VR preserves patient dignity by allowing them to maintain a sense of individuality during recovery, rather than merely feeling like an institutionalized subject.

As each journey to recovery differs between patients, personalized rehabilitation programs with individualized involvement can improve recovery rate. Recent studies in stroke research "suggest that repetitive, task-oriented training" of the affected body areas is effective.[4] However, delivering intense care in the environment of a clinic may be problematic to achieve due to staff limitations. With traditional therapy, "a patient is usually seen for 30 to 45 minutes twice a day in a hospital or rehabilitation center" which impedes the proper time requirement of patient-specific attention required for rehabilitation.[5] On the contrary, VR technology has the power to fabricate a rehabilitation environment "enhanced to create the most appropriate, individualized motor learning approach".[5] The integration of merely 20 minutes of VR games as therapy "frees up 33% of a physical therapist's time" within rehabilitation sessions.1 The valuable resource of a physical therapist's attention can then be reallocated efficiently to patients who may require aid for more severe conditions. The patient therefore assumes a more active, independent role in recovery which may boost their psychological confidence.

Aside from the practical applications of VR technology, this alternative rehabilitation technique can drastically impact the emotional states of patients. An integral portion of the rehabilitation process not only lies in the healing of the physical body but of the mind as well. According to a study by Lange and Flynn (2015), VR gaming technology has allowed patients to view treatment with a more engaging approach and excited mindset.[6] While they can be effective for recovery, traditional therapy exercises typically comprise of basic, repetitive motions which merit "poor engagement and lack of interest by patients".[1] In comparison, VR games—which were originally designed for entertainment—provide the rare opportunity to experience an augmented three-dimensional world. Activities are typically more enjoyable in comparison to traditional methods, causing many patients to "wor[k] harder than [they] would have in normal therapy".[6]

Moreover, VR therapy acts as a positive distraction for patients during recovery. Participants have noted that the modern rehabilitation strategy "gave [them] confidence" to perform weight transfer activities, which are often major roadblocks to stroke balance recovery.[6] By shifting focus to an alternative goal, patients can concentrate on merely winning a game or setting a new score rather than dwelling on the strenuous (and potentially painful) exercises. According to patient testimony, the VR game medium reduced their fear and inspired them to take further steps to rehabilitation.[6]

Combined, these aspects of VR treatment were found to "encourage higher numbers of repetitions" of treatment exercises.[7] Therefore, VR can motivate patients to engage in an increasingly active role in their recovery. Stroke rehabilitation is a long-term journey; without a strong sense of determination to self-improve, healing is extremely difficult.

The current state of knowledge in stroke rehabilitation advocates the value of traditional therapy, with research showing that it "can help regain motor function and ameliorate disability".[4] However, studies exist with evidence showing that when compared side-by-side, VR therapy was the more promising technique. A six-week balance training program hosted by the Department of Physical Therapy in the Bukbu Hospital of Seoul, South Korea, resulted in stroke patients receiving VR therapy "show[ing] a more significant improvement than the [traditional therapy] group" in multiple balance tests.[3] Furthermore, Yang and Hwang (2011) found that "VR treadmill training also improves balance skill…and the involvement of the paretic limb in level walking more than traditional treadmill training does".[8]

Although VR therapy offers these improvements to the field of stroke balance rehabilitation, it has flaws that pose barriers to its implementation. The study and consequent proof of VR therapy rehabilitative ability are limited.[4] The current healthcare system favours traditional rehabilitation methods which, as seen above, have historically proven to be effective to date. Without ample research-proven evidence, therapists face difficulty in finding the material to illuminate the value of modern VR. Convincing peers and governments across the globe to fund the implementation of new technology may become a significant challenge.[4]

Furthermore, VR therapy is limited in its ability to affect all people. Most studies have observed patients of mild to moderate conditions to draw data; those who have severe strokes may be rendered unable to meet the minimal requirement of conscious movement needed to participate in the gaming technology.[2] Stroke patients also experience diverse types and locations of injury which may or may not be applicable to VR therapy. Additionally, patients, especially of old age, may be unwilling to delve into the world of unfamiliar technology. Conventional, therapist-dependent rehabilitation methods may provide more comfort in their recovery journeys.[2]

Finally, depending on the level of immersive equipment needed for rehabilitation, implementation of VR technology may pose logistical complications in clinics and higher expenses in health care. Simple video gaming technologies such as the Wii Fit Board system are inexpensive, costing approximately $50 to $100 CAD per console and require little space.[3,6] However, more advanced systems have higher costs and are therefore not readily available at many clinics whose patients may already face many health care expenses.[3]

Virtual Reality is a computer-based technology that allows users to experience three-dimensional simulations and observe movement with real-time performance feedback.[3] It is a modern development that can be applied to improve balance and motor skills for patients in need of healthcare, with specific benefits towards stroke rehabilitation.[3] When compared to traditional therapy for stroke (which heavily focuses on simple repetitive motions), the pattern of research in the field suggests that VR opens more advanced doors to recovery through both increased practicality of technique and heightened patient psychological engagement.[7] These two strategies of stroke rehabilitation have their own sets of benefits and flaws. However, the relatively few costs of VR are outweighed by its potential benefits to healthcare. Although a knowledge deficit still exists in the field of VR, current evidence suggests that this modern technology may provide promising improvements in stroke rehabilitation for the future of the aging world.

WORKS CITED

Rajaratnam, B. S., et al. "Does the Inclusion of Virtual Reality Games within Conventional Rehabilitation Enhance Balance Retraining after a Recent Episode of Stroke?" *Rehabilitation Research and Practice*, vol. 2013, 2013, pp. 1–6., doi:10.1155/2013/649561

Saposnik, G., and M. Levin. "Virtual Reality in Stroke Rehabilitation: A Meta-Analysis and Implications for Clinicians." *Stroke* 42, no. 5 (2011): 1380-386. doi:10.1161/strokeaha.110.605451.

Cho, Ki Hun, et al. "Virtual-Reality Balance Training with a Video-Game System Improves Dynamic Balance in Chronic Stroke Patients." *The Tohoku Journal of Experimental Medicine*, Tohoku University Medical Press, 30 Aug. 2012, www.jstage.jst.go.jp/article/tjem/228/1/228_69/_article.

Saposnik, G., et al. "Effectiveness of Virtual Reality Using Wii Gaming Technology in Stroke Rehabilitation: A Pilot Randomized Clinical Trial and Proof of Principle." *Stroke*, vol. 41, no. 7, 2010, pp. 1477–1484., doi:10.1161/strokeaha.110.584979.

Merians, Alma S., David Jack, and Rares Boian. "Virtual Reality–Augmented Rehabilitation for Patients Following Stroke." *Physical Therapy* 82, no. 9 (September 01, 2002): 898-915. doi:10.1093/ptj/82.9.898.

Lange, Belinda, Sheryl Flynn, Rachel Proffitt, Chien-Yen Chang, and Albert "Skip" Rizzo. 2010. "Development of an Interactive Game-Based Rehabilitation Tool for Dynamic Balance Training." *Topics in Stroke Rehabilitation* 17 (5): 345–52. doi:10.1310/tsr1705-345.

Laver, K., S. George, S. Thomas, J. E. Deutsch, and M. Crotty. „Virtual Reality for Stroke Rehabilitation." *Stroke* 43, no. 2 (2011). doi:10.1161/strokeaha.111.642439.

Yang, Saiwei, Wei-Hsung Hwang, Yi-Ching Tsai, Fu-Kang Liu, Lin-Fen Hsieh, and Jen-Suh Chern. "Improving Balance Skills in Patients Who Had Stroke Through Virtual Reality Treadmill Training." *American Journal of Physical Medicine & Rehabilitation* 90, no. 12 (December 2011): 969-78. doi:10.1097/phm.0b013e3182389fae.

The Effects and Challenges of Artificial Intelligence in Medicine

Anumeet Chepal

OVER THE PAST two decades, the study of Artificial Intelligence (AI) has made several breakthroughs in research and studies. Some monumental projects include autonomous driving cars, and interactive robots (for example, Amazon's "Alexa," and Apple's "Siri"). With our technological consumption increasing, there are more advances towards AI and programming research. This technology is not only relevant for the average consumer but becoming increasingly important for doctors and medical practitioners. In the public eye, AI and Virtual Reality (VR) can be revolutionary in the medical field. Aside from scholars and scientists, the public's perception of this technology is also positive. The Washington Post recently covered a story explaining how doctors were able to save the lives of newborn conjoined twins using VR technology to build virtual models of their heart, increasing the third dimension image size from the "size of a walnut to the size of an average living room" (Holley, 2017). This incredible advancement in technology had saved the lives of those twins while simultaneously opening the doors to more opportunities and advancements in the medical sector. Artificial Intelligence has affected and addressed the challenges doctors and medical specialists have faced over the past two decades. These improvements include a significant increase of accuracy in medical diagnoses, and providing aid to individuals in developing countries. However, this technology also poses the major threat to society in regards to confidentiality and for scientists, AI's cognitive issues in programming creates hurdles in development.

Artificial Intelligence has also improved the accuracy of medical diagnoses. Scientists, Abbas Sheikhtaheri, Farahnaz Sadoughi, and Zahra Hasemi Dehaghi of the Tehran University of Medical Sciences reviewed and evaluated the uses and accuracy of AI in their paper, "Developing and Using Expert Systems and Neural Networks in Medicine: A Review on Benefits and Challenges". They concluded that "the systems [of Artificial Intelligence had] achieved promising results in medicine" (Sheikhtaheri and Company, 2014). For example, the system was able to "diagnose different types of headaches with 98% accuracy" and "diagnose tuberculosis with 94.88% accuracy", (Sheikhtaheri and Company). It is clear that the technology and its results are reassuring. Although the technology is designed for independent thinking and decision making, its programming regards a limited list of medical matters. Though the current intelligence has the capacity to compute solutions to only basic medical problems, it still proves useful for humans. The potential uses of this knowledge can provide aid for people in developing countries where there is an evident lack of equipment and knowledge.

This technology is incredibly valuable in the medical field as it is more efficient, eliminates the factors of potential human error and is impeccably accurate in crucial measurements and calculations. It would be revolutionary for developing countries with limited medical access and knowledge. These advancements in artificial intelligence, if shared with countries in desperate need of the medical attention and aid, can improve the world's global health and wellbeing ratio. These advancements can be applied for a humanitarian cause and provide assistance and valuable knowledge for countries that are currently lacking that support system.

However, although the benefits of AI in the medical sector are remarkable, they do raise certain issues that require an equal amount (if not more) attention. According to the panel discussion at the Artificial Intelligence in Medicine Europe (AIME) conference held in July 2007, "The general AI research community [is] fascinated by the applications being developed in the medical world, noting that significant new AI methods were emerging as AIM researchers struggled with challenging... problems." (Vimla L. Patel, 2007). At the conference, Peter Szolovits of the Computer Science and Artificial Intelligence Laboratory at the Massachusetts Institute of Technology stated, "Much latent resistance to fully electronic tracking of health care arises from people's unfortunately correct beliefs that aggregation of vast amounts of sensitive healthcare data increases vulnerability to massive disclosures." (Szolovits, 2007). Ten years later his statement is still proven to stand true. There are incredibly high risks with digitizing all medical records of every citizen. If this sensitive information were to be leaked or hacked, then it would result in a horrible violation of privacy and contribute to a negative image for AI in the medical industry. Szolovits adds that "We need convenient and secure means of authentication, better than today's username/password combinations, whether by personal smart cards, biometrics, or some clever exploitation of already-existing technologies that can serve to identify people, such as their credit cards or cellular phones." His thoughts are still current as even technological specialists still struggle with the far too frequent intrusions of privacy.

Another common issue that is recurring while programming AI technology is entering data and facts into the database, however, lacking the actual knowledge and expertise to apply it. Riccardo Bellazzi (of the University of Pavia) and Ameen Abu-Hanna (of the University of Amsterdam) both claim that "Scientists working in a "data-driven world" are recognizing the strong risk of concentrating on data gathering and analysis alone," (Bellazzi and Company, 2007). They then go on to say that the "[programming of] decision-making may overlook the importance of research on complex planning, decision-making under uncertainty, and individual risk management," (Bellazzi and Company). This, although a popular problem, is still relevant and pressing for scientists. In order to create AI technology that is able to fully deliver a wide range of medical services and information, it must be able to apply its knowledge to any possible outcome.

Despite its current limitations, the possibilities and applications of artificial intelligence in medicine are boundless. Based on the information available and discussed by academic scholars today, this technology is crucial towards the improvement of medicinal practices and humanity as a whole. AI not only improves the accuracy and limits the variables in testing and diagnoses, but it could also serve for humanitarian causes too. AI technology, if applied to the areas and people in the world that are desperately in need of this medical attention, could increase overall global health. The side effects of this technology, however, need to be addressed by scientific scholars and society. For scientists, the issue of programming techniques that can apply a plethora of information to an infinite number outcomes is a progressing challenge. As for developers and society, the issue of privacy and confidentiality is yet to be seriously addressed. The world's medical history is a sensitive matter and should be regarded as such. Past the challenges and issues that artificial intelligence raises, this technology can be lifesaving and has the potential to revolutionize the world of medicine, and of course, global health.

WORKS CITED

Holley, P., & Holley, P. (2017). *How doctors used virtual reality to save the lives of conjoined twin sisters. Washington Post.* Retrieved 28 November 2017, from https://www.washingtonpost.com/news/innovations/wp/2017/07/21/how-doctors-used-virtual-reality-to-save-the-lives-of-conjoined-twin-sisters/?utm_ term=.2d0cd85a6be2

Patel, V., Shortliffe, E., Stefanelli, M., Szolovits, P., Berthold, M., Bellazzi, R., & Abu-Hanna, A. (2009). The coming of age of artificial intelligence in medicine. *Artificial Intelligence In Medicine, 46*(1), 5–17. http://dx.doi.org/10.1016/j. artmed.2008.07.017

Sheikhtaheri, A., Sadoughi, F., & Hashemi Dehaghi, Z. (2014). Developing and Using Expert Systems and Neural Networks in Medicine: A Review on Benefits and Challenges. *Journal Of Medical Systems, 38*(9). http://dx.doi.org/10.1007/ s10916-014-0110-5

Virtual Reality Therapy Incorporating All Psychotherapies

Jennifer Dong

IN THE PAST, there have been debates over which form of psychotherapy is best. Cognitive Behavioural Therapy (CBT) has been in the running for being superior out of all the other non-CBT therapies. Norcross and Newman have described this ongoing argument as, "In the infancy of the field, therapy systems, like battling siblings, competed for attention and affection in a "dogma eat dogma" environment… Mutual antipathy and exchange of puerile insults between the adherents of rival orientations were much the order of the day," (Norcross and Newman, p. 3). In an article by David F. Tolin, he compares CBT with other non-CBT therapies such as psychodynamic, interpersonal, and supportive therapies ruling out that CBT is better for certain conditions but it should not be revered as above all (Tolin, 710). On the other hand, Timothy P. Baardseth notes that no matter what type of disorder it is, the effectiveness of CBT and non-CBT treatments are similar (Baardseth, 395). Virtual Reality Therapy (VRT) can put all the debates to rest because VRT may be able to imitate all therapeutic methods.

One of the first scholarly works to address the topic of which therapy is better was by Tolin. His research stated that "the superiority of CBT over alternative therapies was evident only among patients with anxiety or depressive disorders," (Tolin, 710). Tolin collected many articles and data and organized their information based on a series of steps. To ensure that all articles were under the same breath, they had to be bona fide treatments. He defined bona fide treatments as psychotherapies that, "…are (a) delivered by trained therapists and (b) based on psychological principles, (c) offered to the psychotherapy community as books or manuals, or (d) contained specified components. Therefore, a treatment was considered bona fide if criterion (a) and at least one of the criteria (b), (c), or (d) was met," (Tolin, 713). After excluding articles that were not bona fide treatments, Tolin analysed the data "using Comprehensive Meta-Analysis v.2.2 software, with supplemental analyses conducted using SPSS v.15" (Tolin, 713). He also used a variable named,

Cohen's d, which indicates the difference in effectiveness between CBT and non-CBT treatments. After measuring many other variables, Tolin concluded that "CBT outperforms other forms of psychotherapy at post-treatment" (Tolin, 718). He stated that CBT may be more suitable for depressive and anxiety disorders but not always superior to alternative treatment methods.

Three years later, Timothy P. Baardseth reanalysed Tolin's study and proved that "there were no differences between CBT treatments and bona fide non-CBT treatments across disorder-specific and non-disorder specific symptom measures," (Baardseth, 395). This meant that it does not matter whether it is an anxiety and/or depressive disorder because all treatments produced similar results. Baardseth supported his argument by tackling Tolin's distinction of what constitutes a CBT treatment. Baardseth noted, "Tolin classified a treatment as CBT if it contained any of the following components: relaxation training (including progressive muscle relaxation, meditation, or breathing retraining), exposure therapy (imaginal or in vivo exposure, including flooding and implosive therapy), behavior rehearsal (behavioral training in social skills, habit reversal, or problem solving), cognitive restructuring (including direct strategies to identify and alter maladaptive thought processes), or operant procedures (systematic manipulation of reinforcers or punishers for behavior, including behavioral activation)," (Baardseth, 397). He stated that this categorization incorporated too many components into a very big scope. Second, he said that Tolin's research "considered only disorder-specific (i.e., targeted) symptom measures for depression and anxiety" (Baardseth, 397). This implied that Tolin did not cover the other end of the spectrum. Baardseth then did his own research with the intention of "evaluating the relative efficacy of bona fide CBT treatments to bona fide non-CBT treatment" (Baardseth, 399). The first step to his research was to select published studies based on clinical trials and filter out studies that did not meet detailed criteria he set. For example, one of the many criteria the studies had to meet was that it must compare both CBT and non-CBT treatment (Baardseth, 399). Next, Baardseth had five psychology doctoral students sort and collect only the bona fide treatments. He defined bona fide treatments differently compared to Tolin because he cited a definition from another author as "those that were delivered by trained therapists and were based on psychological principles, were offered to the psychotherapy community as viable treatments (e.g., through professional books or manuals), or contained specified components" (Wampold, Mondin, Moody, Stich, et al., 1997, p. 205). Similar to Tolin, he compared variables. In Baardseth's case, it was the Q value: it presents differences in effect sizes as well as homogeneity (Baardseth, 402). He wrote, "For the disorder-specific measures, the Q statistic was significant ($Q[12]=35.73$, $p=.004$), which indicated there was significant between-study heterogeneity," and continues, "Similarly for non-disorder specific measures, the Q statistic was also significant ($Q[11]=54.64$, pb.001)," (Baardseth, 401-402). After he compared CBT to non-CBT treatments, his results proved that CBT was not superior compared to other treatments because his findings showed "roughly 69% of the variability in the observed effect was due to true between-study variability" (Baardseth, 402).

How can VRT pose a solution by imitating all these different treatment methods? Some of the therapies researched above are CBT, interpersonal, and/or supportive. CBT is prolonged exposure therapy to scenarios that are anxiety-provoking. CBT teaches patients how to think about their fears and develop more rational behaviours/responses to stimuli. Based on an article by E. Klinger titled Virtual Reality Versus Cognitive Behaviour Therapy for Social Phobia: A Preliminary Controlled Study demonstrated that VRT has the same effect and results as CBT. In one of Klinger's experiment in the VR group, there were a total of five different kinds of environments. All of these environments are similar to CBT in the sense that they expose the user to situations that will trigger their anxiety. Klinger says, "The user learns how to move forward and backward, how to look up, down and around, how to open doors, and how to sit on a chair in front of a television set," (Klinger, 80) before proceeding with the actual therapy. In one experiment, "The user learns to speak in front of a public audience. The storyboard takes place in a meeting room where the user joins seven other participants who are already sitting and speaking around a big table," (Klinger, 80). Having the user speak to an audience will trigger their anxiety which is essentially what CBT aims to do. During the "assessment" exposure, the therapist kept tabs on the user asking questions such as, "What thoughts do you have?" (Klinger, 82) to see how they will cope. Klinger's results have demonstrated that the difference in effectiveness between VRT and CBT are negligible.

Interpersonal therapy deals with the dynamics of the patient's relationships with friends and families. This type of therapy works on self-awareness and communication skills. For instance, most professionals use interpersonal therapy for patients suffering from depression, relationship problems, and postpartum depression. VRT can simulate this by displaying visuals of the friends or families they are having problems with, thus allowing them to actually speak their minds and act without having fears holding them back.

Supportive therapy is when the professional becomes an outlet for the patient to vent to. The role of the professional is to listen, advise, reassure, etc. VRT can model this by having a scenario where the patient is asked to confront a digital image of their own self and give them advice based on their own issues and feelings. This will engage the patient more because they are playing the role of the patient as well as the therapist.

Virtual Reality (VR) is a growing resource that immerses users into a digital world. All different types of psychotherapy treatments ranging from CBT, interpersonal, supportive, etc., could potentially be all categorized under VRT, subduing all the disputes over which treatment is best.

WORKS CITED

Baardseth, Timothy P., et al. "Cognitive-behavioral therapy versus other therapies: Redux." *Clinical Psychology Review* 33.3 (2013): 395-405.

Harris, Sandra R., Robert L. Kemmerling, and Max M. North. "Brief virtual reality therapy for public speaking anxiety." *Cyberpsychology & behavior* 5.6 (2002): 543–550.

Klinger, Evelyne, et al. "Virtual reality therapy versus cognitive behavior therapy for social phobia: A preliminary controlled study." *Cyberpsychology & behavior* 8.1 (2005): 76–88.

"Mental Health and Psychotherapy." *WebMD*, WebMD, www.webmd.com/mental-health/mental-health-psychotherapy.

Neuman, Fredric. "Supportive Psychotherapy." *Psychology Today*, Sussex Publishers, 2 June 2013, www.psychologytoday.com/blog/fighting-fear/201306/supportive-psychotherapy

Tolin, David F. "Is cognitive–behavioral therapy more effective than other therapies?: A meta-analytic review." *Clinical psychology review* 30.6 (2010): 710–720.

Reimagining the Harsh Reality of Anxiety in VR

Robert Hebert

THE PROSPECT OF showcasing work to a room full of peers is often a frightening one. This familiar sentiment was echoed by myself and multiple peers in a First-Year Seminar in Science (SCIE 113) class taken last year. A respectable portion of our grade hinged on interviewing a research scientist and presenting insights into their academic role, research methods, and contributions to science. Leading up to the presentation, the all-too-convenient piece of advice we received was that "it gets better with practice." Exposure therapy seems to agree, asserting that continued, incremental, non-dangerous exposure to phobias and sources of anxiety is the path to treating them. Couple that with the notion that VR can bridge the gap between rehearsed exposures and "the real thing", and it becomes clear why VR might be a promising practice alternative to the mirror. "Affective outcomes of virtual reality exposure therapy for anxiety and specific phobias: A meta-analysis" (Parsons & Rizzo, 2008) analyzes the effectiveness of this very topic, and Kwon, Powell, and Chalmers further entertain this idea as it applies to job interviews in "How level of realism influences anxiety in virtual reality environments for a job interview" (2013). To handle presentation anxiety in much the same way, however, might not be a fully developed solution. Preparing students to handle their presentation anxiety is an undeniably important niche to fill, but the literature on its therapy usage suggests that VR has a more important role in reinventing the "presentation" altogether.

Exposure therapy has a fixation on gradually approaching realism, a framework that also marks its approach to VR. It stems from the neurological concept that to rewire a patient's fear reaction to a stimulus, that same stimulus needs to be activated in the therapy condition (Parsons & Rizzo, 2008). If we apply this principle to virtual environments, there is no choice but to strive for immersion through photorealism and multisensory feedback. Kwon et al. (2013)'s first experiment, in which subjects are interviewed in VR by computer models with different levels of visual detail, aligns very much with this design idea. The demonstrated effect here is that increasing the polygon level of a perceived "social actor", or how detailed the interviewer's character model looks, induces more symptoms associated with anxiety (Kwon et al., 2013). VR exposure therapy would then seem to welcome any breakthroughs that allow higher visual detail, crisper sound, tactile feedback, or anything of the like. To stimulate the patient with increasing likeness to the real thing should, in theory, better prepare patients for encountering the real thing.

It is not inconceivable that fear of presentations and job interviews might be wholly different from other phobias. Exposure therapy depends on the ability of the brain to control fear responses by self-adjustment, so while it is helpful to describe these effects in terms of stimuli and changing brain states, therein lies the very problem (Parsons and Rizzo, 2008). Parsons and Rizzo (2008) were able to demonstrate, in their statistical analysis of many types of VR exposure therapy, that the anxiety reduction effect is more potent for basic fears. Aviophobia and agoraphobia, the fear of flight and entrapment in unsafe environments respectively, ranked among the highest mean anxiety reduction effects (Parsons and Rizzo, 2008). These two fears are decidedly easier stimuli to present to subjects. To stimulate a user as if they are flying is to show them the interior of an airplane with a VR headset and possibly introduce "turbulence" through a chair. Social interactions prove to be a different beast. Kwon et al. (2013) readily admit in their conclusion that their study is limited both by the inability to measure social anxiety reliably and that social anxiety is not just a perceptual stimulus. The thought of being watched while presenting or interviewing is less grounded in the idea of perceptual stimuli than being on a plane or seeing a bug and is tangled in a web of complex social constructs. When a stimulus is more than just an environment a virtual environment might not be providing the whole therapeutic picture.

The issue at hand then becomes not one of how we better adjust students to present in real-life conditions, but why these conditions are so important to emulate in the first place. Presentations delivered conventionally are ascribed some sense of normality, which is wholly undue considering this task proves more convenient in virtual reality. This is arguably the crux of VR research in this area: that VR exposure is designed to be a set of less-horrible steps up to the "real thing" because we can control what is seemingly "missing" from the experience. It seems valuable that Kwon et al. (2013) mention simulating eye contact in their interviewer avatar, for example, as it deepens immersion. This creates the effect of the avatar being a "social actor", whose involvement in the conversation creates the same physiological effects (e.g. sweating, shaky hands, self-reported nervousness) (Kwon et al., 2013). To simply relegate VR to simulations of real life like that, however, is to ignore its power to be inventive. It is possible the job interview and the presentation are problematic scenarios, to begin with, and it is okay that aspects are "missing" in VR. In an example scenario where every student rehearsed their presentation wholly in VR, there is little justification for not actually presenting in a virtual classroom as well. Does this VR environment have to simulate real life or is this something we require because it is familiar? Being watched by 30 pairs of eyes brings hardly any value added from the presenter's point of view, and VR, by nature of being constructed virtually, can allow that the presenter sees the most comfortable image of the audience while the audience can observe all aspects of the presenter. Kwon et al. (2013) focus on slowly growing accustomed to the "default" mode of communication, that being speaking in-person. In many cases, however, being actually present in the same room may not equate to a better presentation. We can even entertain the idea that the presentation need not be confined to slides on a projector in a classroom, and instead include 360-degree panoramas of a lab or a research station for presentation's sake. The presentation could be recorded from multiple angles if that helps the marking process. A class assignment is entirely teacher-constructed, so presentation anxiety is a fear that can be addressed by changing guidelines as opposed to requiring every student learn to present in a dated form. Conventional reality does not need to be the default mode of presentation if it proves worse in comparison.

The idea that VR is merely practice for real life when real life gets too uncomfortable is an extremely limited one. The fact that students are expected to prepare for conventional presentations at all should seem counterintuitive, other than the fact that it is a familiar art and already so entrenched in course curricula. Virtual reality redefines what is "real", in a sense, and the very real concept of a presentation is up for renegotiation. It is ironic that the most immediate answer to handling social fears is to practice them with the very devices that can deconstruct these fears altogether. The convenient rhetoric that Powerpoint presentations are a necessary evil for communicating science then seems dated when that evil is not so obviously necessary.

Kwon, J. H., Powell, J., & Chalmers, A. (2013). How level of realism influences anxiety in virtual reality environments for a job interview. *International Journal of Human-Computer Studies, 71*(10), 978–987. doi:10.1016/j.ijhcs.2013.07.003

Parsons, T. D., & Rizzo, A. A. (2008). Affective outcomes of virtual reality exposure therapy for anxiety and specific phobias: A meta-analysis. *Journal of Behavior Therapy and Experimental Psychiatry, 39*(3), 250–261. doi:10.1016/j.jbtep.2007.07.007

Implementing Virtual Reality into Healthcare Education in order to Decrease Mortality Rates caused by Medical Error

Neriyel Reyes

THE HEALTH CARE system has increasingly advanced to prioritize the importance of quality and safety of all health care members, especially those of the patients. Despite positive advancements in health care techniques, human and systematic errors are factors that continue to contribute to the death rate. Even as far as thirty years ago, medical accidents such as preventable human error have reportedly been one of the leading causes of death (C.A. Vincent, 1989). The practice of medicine is indeed a less than perfect process, however, "there [were] a limited number of studies in the healthcare professional literature related to medical error disclosure." [Stroud et al., 2013] That being said, it is not enough for members in the healthcare system to adopt ways of preventing erroneous circumstances, but to also report and know how to manage those inevitable human errors.

One proposal to address the negligence of medical error and the lack of disclosing such errors is to construct a simulation of medical circumstances via virtual reality (VR). The convenience of computer simulation can be utilized to interactively guide pre-medicine students and professionals through the process of tending to their patients, paying particular attention to limiting any medical errors. Supplementary to this, virtual reality can imitate a situation where the participant, in this case, the student, can be tested on their intuition and adaptability to handle errors that have already occurred, in a virtual, risk-free environment (Caylor et al., 2015). The engineering of VR can accommodate the many possible cases where medical errors can occur, and thus be prevented when applied to real life.

The first step in avoiding medical error is to understand that there are numerous factors that contribute to human and systematic mistakes. Such factors often involve the faults of the drug provider organization, or even the imperfections of the medication-use system itself (Aspden et al., in Committee on Identifying and Preventing Medication Errors Board on Health Care Services). It is often found that multiple underlying factors are involved in medical miscommunication, and not the fault of a single individual. This was the case in 1996, where a hospital in Denver confirmed that a "medication error had led to the death of a day-old infant, born to a mother with a prior history of syphilis" [Aspden et al., 2000]. An initial aspect that led to an eventual downfall of the medical procedure was that both parents were only able to speak Spanish, thus her past treatment and current status (of herself and the infant) was not confirmed; regardless the hospital decided to treat the baby with congenital (inherited from birth) syphilis anyhow. Further miscommunication ensued when the infectious disease specialists recorded a dose of 'Benzathine penicillin G 150,000U IM (U = "units", IM = "intramuscularly") to be ordered, but the hospital's pharmacist, "having limited knowledge about the drug," [43] prescribed a dosage of 1,500,000 units IM, misinterpreting the letter U as a leading zero from the original 150,000 units. This erroneous ten-fold amount exceeds the injection standard for infants, causing, the nurse practitioners to administer the drug intravenously (IV) as opposed to via muscularly (IM), in order to reduce "pain to the infant with the large IM injection dose." [44.] Benzathine penicillin G is an insoluble drug, blocking the blood flow into the lungs if injected intravenously, thus the infant became unresponsive after administration of 1.8 mL (Aspden et al., 2000). The autopsy concluded that the infant did not inherit syphilis from the mother, thus, diagnosing and treating the baby with congenital syphilis should not have occurred initially. Upon careful analysis of this medical tragedy, it is apparent that because the medical staff is governed by the healthcare system within which they act, the underlying causes of the errors belong to the system; where the mistakes lie outside the control of the individuals (Aspden et al., pp 45).

As seen by one of many negligent medical fatalities, it is evident that explicit communication in the healthcare workforce is a crucial factor that ensures patient safety. According to The Institute of Medicine (2011), education beyond the traditional learning environment is necessary in order to maximize the application of skills, notably, effective teamwork via communication. Considering that there are so little studies found that improve communication-based on disclosing error (Stroud et al., 2013), a revolutionary approach such as virtual reality (VR), would touch upon both interactive education and collaborative skill sets (Baker et al., 2008), ultimately decreasing the number of lethal medical errors. Adopting virtual simulation into the healthcare education is an effective means of interprofessional collaborative training; that is, where two or more different professional disciplines collaborate to work towards a common goal (Popkess et al, 2017). In support of interprofessional education, Caylor et al's interprofessional virtual clinical simulation (Volume 11, Issue 3), concluded that students favoured Second Life® (brand name of VR simulation) as an effective platform for multi-professional learning, where the virtual simulation reduced stress levels and provided confidence all while offering a realistic approach to patient care (Caylor et al., 2015). Provided that the field of medicine has "progressed into an increasingly complex and specialty-driven system," [Popkess et al., pp 574] it is practical to implement the adaptive technological nature of VR to further advance the evolution of science. These advantages of virtual reality come forth particularly in the healthcare education, where its dynamic mechanism can be suitable to train and prevent medical staff from causing errors in a continuously evolving and highly experimental discipline of medicine.

The development of a collaborative and successful medical staff unit is a key foundation for providing safe and effective patient-centered care (Meleis et al., 2016); In order to develop this foundation, interprofessional education (IPE) can be implemented in the healthcare system by use of virtual reality to improve the attitude on communicating and disclosing medical accidents. According to the Institute of Medicine (2000), greater than 100,000 patients per year suffer from reported medical errors. Although there are clear ethical guidelines stated in health care providers, "health professionals often fear disclosing errors […] in fear of possible legal repercussions," (Popkess et al., 2017) and training in disclosing medical error is still not widespread in health education in the United States. Thus, an emphasis on the practice of reporting medical errors to patients is an important factor when implementing virtual reality. IPE via virtual reality provides healthcare students with realistic exposure to situations that can enhance their communication and delivery skills alongside acknowledging their respect for individuals in other disciplines, essentially teaching them to be the best care team member they can be (Careau et al., 2014). This was executed by Sharon Wilson of the University of Washington's case study simulation, held in the spring of 2015 at the University of Washington's Center for Health Sciences Interprofessional Research. The simulation consisted of 202 healthcare students from dental medicine, pharmacy, and nursing, who were then randomly assigned to interprofessional teams of fifteen to twenty members (Popkess et al., 2017). Each team was required to disclose medical errors to three standardized families, each of which reacted in an angry, relieved and depressed manner. The study concluded that the simulation program appeared to be successful in enhancing knowledge and most measured attitudes about error disclosure." [pp 579] An additional study was held where a mock patient case was simulated to "focus on communication, rather than discipline-specific skill." [Caylor et al., 2015 pp 165] The basis of the case included an adult patient with dementia from a nursing home that had been diagnosed with pneumonia. However, the patient "was given a contraindicated medication, and the patient subsequently developed an anaphylactic reaction." [165] Prior to the simulation, each student was provided procedural information of the patient's medical conditions, however, each student deliberately did not receive the exact same details. This, of course, would not be the case in real life situations, where it would be favorable for all staff members to be aware of the patient's full details. The advantage of Wilson's and Popkess' virtual studies provided a harmless teaching opportunity for students where they were "required to communicate and share information [in order] to understand the complete patient story." [Popkess et al., pp 165]

After the simulations were carried out, a positive consensus was concluded. Both virtual reality simulations allowed for a successful training platform with students that resulted in "improved knowledge and attitudes with teamwork and error disclosure." [Popkess et al., 2015] Therefore, it can be beneficial to employ virtual clinical simulations in the future, where participants can bring into practice the communication skills they developed into real life circumstances, fundamentally improving the quality of healthcare services by reducing medical related errors.

WORKS CITED

Aspden, Philip et al. "Preventing Medication Errors." *The National Academies Press,* *2007,* http://perpustakaan.stik-avicenna.ac.id/wp-content/uploads/2014/11/ Preventing-Medication-Error.pdf.

Caylor, Shandra et al. "The Use of Virtual Simulation and a Modified TeamSTEPPS™ Training for Multiprofessional Education." *Elsevier, March 2015,* http://www. sciencedirect.com.ezproxy.library.ubc.ca/science/article/pii/S1876139914002370.

Popkess, Ann et al. "Interprofessional Error Disclosure Simulation for Health Professional Students." *Elsevier, November 2017,* http://www.sciencedirect.com. ezproxy.library.ubc.ca/science/article/pii/S1876139916302365.

Baker, C. et al. "Simulation in interprofessional education for patient-centered collaborative care." *Journals of Advanced Nursing,* 1 September. 2008, pp 372–379, http://dx.doi.org.ezproxy.library.ubc.ca/10.1111/j.1365-2648.2008.04798.x.

Stroud, L. et al. "Teaching medical error disclosure to physicians-in-training: A scope review." *Academic Medicine,* 2013, pp. 884–891.

Augmented Reality and Virtual Reality: Training Surgeons

Devon Hayek

THE MEDICAL FIELD lacks surgical training platforms which are both cost-effective and renewable. Many of the educational tasks novice surgeons face do not directly benefit their performance on patients. Reading instructions out of a textbook may not seem related to the actual surgeries they will be performing in the future. Once these doctors in training reach a high enough prestige to operate on donated body parts, the cost of their practice grows exponentially. Virtual reality and augmented reality technologies provide an alternate route to learning all of the techniques necessary and offer a platform in which surgeons can practice their skills at a fraction of the cost. The experience these instruments provide is much more interactive and relates better to the tasks surgeons perform on a daily basis. Augmented reality and virtual reality are leading technologies in the medical field that assist in educating and training surgeons due to their interactivity and realistic portrayal of surgery.

Augmented reality is an effective tool to help educate novice surgeons as well as experienced professionals in the medical field. This technology can be used to enhance techniques used in medicine, especially for educational purposes. The images collected via magnetic resonance imaging (MRI), computed tomography scans (CT scans) and ultrasound imaging can be rendered and stitched together to form a complete three-dimensional computerized image (Azuma, 356). This image can be transmitted to an augmented reality device, such as the Microsoft HoloLens, and can be superimposed upon the physical patient in real time. In doing so, the surgeon gains so-called "X-ray vision" and can view what lies beneath the skin of the body (Azuma, 356). By allowing the doctor to view the external body and internal body simultaneously, novice surgeons can become more familiar with the body by associating internal systems with the external anatomy of humans. Being able to view an entire human at a time can also allow doctors to gain more information on a patient, as some information can only be viewed with the naked eye and other can only be viewed through imaging devices. Surgeons in training can gain a new perspective by using augmented reality in their studies, which can assist them with using less invasive techniques in surgery. It can also display how systems of the body are interrelated and can be affected by different surgical strategies.

Many different programs to teach surgeons have been created upon the introduction of augmented reality. A project called "HoloBrain" in the Emerging Media Lab at the University of British Columbia has been working on creating the software to project images of the brain using augmented reality technologies. Their goal is to take medical images of a patient brain and use the Microsoft HoloLens to emit a three-dimensional image that can be used for educational purposes. Multiple people can view the image at the same time, which allows for conversation and teaching to occur. The technology of HoloBrain is interactive and can use simple gestures to highlight a particular region of the brain for further analysis. The main purpose of HoloBrain is to allow medical students to become familiar with the brain before moving on to performing crucial surgeries.

Augmented reality can be used as a cost-effective means of surgical practice before acting on a patient. By allowing surgeons to practice a particular procedure multiple times in augmented reality, surgeons can gain helpful motor skills and can memorize different techniques before performing in the operating room for the first time (McCoy, 913). Having the opportunity to practice a procedure also creates a sense of confidence within the student, which is important in the medical field. Augmented and virtual reality gives the unique opportunity for medical students to see the effects their surgery has on a patient. Many different surgical techniques can be tested with this software and can give the results of the metaphorical procedure in real time. In doing so, surgeons can discover the most effective and least invasive techniques when performing a surgery. This also prevents surgical practice on humans. Augmented reality technology also poses the ability for surgeons to be critiqued on their techniques, leading to improvements over time. The MIST System (Minimally Invasive Surgical Trainer System) utilizes augmented reality as well as two surgical hands "for training and assessment of surgical laparoscopic psychomotor skills" (McCloy, 913). It allows a doctor to perform certain tasks using the two hands, which appear on a screen in real time. The program can train professionals on a plethora of different surgical operations. The MIST system is calibrated to know the most economical techniques of surgery in different situations and can then use this calibration to determine the amount of experience a surgeon has. It can detect trembles from the surgeon as well as recognize accuracy and errors with the procedure (McCloy, 914). The system also tracks the amount of time it takes the user to complete a task and compares it with the optimal duration of the surgery. Following the simulated surgery, the doctor receives a score and can view areas of improvement. With this given feedback, medical professionals can perfect their dexterity by repeating this process over and over until the MIST system detects high accuracy in their technique. Studies have determined that "training on a simulator has been shown to translate into performance in the operating room" (McCloy, 914), which strengthens the need for these training devices. Augmented reality training devices lack the realism of the operating room and need another dimension in order to simulate reality.

In contrast to augmented reality, virtual reality simulators utilize the effect of telepresence to create the illusion of residing within an operating room while practicing surgery. By using virtual reality technology, the novice doctor can get a more realistic sense of working within the operating room while having the ability to appear to be using different surgical tools in real time. In an educational sense, virtual reality is advantageous as the steps of the surgery can be projected in the virtual world, allowing the doctor to refrain from referring to a manual during practice sessions (Azuma, 357). A virtual reality company called OSSO VR has brought virtual reality to operating room training. The software that they have created allows for realistic hands-on surgical training that is cost-effective and avoids practicing on humans. OSSO VR can be used to increase the dexterity and confidence of surgeons and is portable. Being portable, surgeons can practice their techniques in a multitude of locations while hauling a light load. The program also uses headphones to simulate the sounds heard during surgery. The headset can also be used to receive instructions from an external source, who may be an instructor assisting or testing the surgeon in training. By using OSSO VR, surgical innovation is encouraged as new techniques can be easily introduced to novice doctors. Virtual reality technology is crucial in creating a platform in which surgeons can practice their skills and have a seamless transition entering the operating room.

Augmented reality allows for surgeons in training to investigate and learn more about the body, by projecting superimposed scans on a physical human body and by creating practice platforms. It can assist in determining the fitness of a surgeon for a task by evaluating their skills prior to an operation. Augmented reality has the unique ability for many people to view the same images in real time, allowing for educational use in the medical field. Virtual reality, on the other hand, creates an immersive world by means of telepresence to better represent the operating room in a three-dimensional sense. This method creates more room for surgeons to learn new techniques and memorize the procedural steps associated with a specific operation. Augmented reality and virtual reality are both utilized in medicine to allow doctors to better understand the anatomy of humans as well as practice procedures at a low cost, which is extremely beneficial for novice surgeons.

WORKS CITED

Azuma, Ronald T. "A Survey of Augmented Reality." *Presence: Teleoperators & Virtual Environments*, vol. 6, no. 4, 1997, pp. 355–385.

McCloy, Rory, and Robert Stone. "Science, Medicine, and the Future: Virtual Reality in Surgery." *BMJ: British Medical Journal*, vol. 323, no. 7318, 2001, pp. 912–915.

Can Virtual Reality Transfer Laparoscopic Surgical Skills to the Operating Room?

Matthew Parnian

INTRODUCTION

SURGERY IS A BRANCH of medical practice that treats the body with manual and instrumental techniques. Medicine continues to present the underlying complications of moral and ethical issues that reduces available resources, which subsequently impedes the growth of novice surgeons as medical professionals. The refinement and development of surgical skills is sought after globally, and with the advancement of technology, interdisciplinary research allows for the implementation of computer simulations in newer methods of teaching surgery.

Laparoscopy is a minimally invasive and accessible operation performed through small incisions with the aid of a camera. This method of surgery imposes a lower level of risk on the patient and allows for minimal wound exposure; however, this method requires an excessive amount of training and practice to perform successfully, as the surgeon has limited access (Seymour et al., 2002). Laparoscopy is a practice that has many transferable skills, combined with the long procedural time, is a notable operation to perform tests to determine different methods of training. Surgical schools continue to use clinical practice on real patients, but the incorporation of a newer technology, such as an operating theater, using virtual reality can assist the transfer of surgical efficiency, and technical skills to real life practices in the operating room (Larsen et al., 2009).

SURGICAL EFFICIENCY

Surgical efficiency is a skill which is practiced to primarily reduce surgical trauma, to allow for faster postoperative recovery, and offer shorter hospital stays (Larsen et al., 2009). Decision making efficiency and the transfer of the skill to clinical environments with real operations is cognitive skill influenced by psychology (Larsen et al., 2009), as it involves the aspects of familiariz-ation and independent thinking without supervisor influence. Subjects who have operated through virtual reality have encountered the exact situation in a simulation and have adapted to the situations presented in laparoscopic oper-ations; however, during clinical trainings, the subjects are more cautious of their situation, as they are aware of the living animal or human they are train-ing on (Larsen et al., 2009). Simulators ultimately teach judgement, as sur-geons are no longer dependent on teacher determined instructions, rather a dynamic and interactive process which teaches problem solving and decision making as the individual interacts in real-time (Seymour et al. 2002). In com-parison, clinical training is often done while shadowing a superior or super-vised by an invigilator, making it difficult to take initiative and learn through trial and error independently (Seymour et al., 2002). Surgeons who train on virtual reality are expected to perform better than clinically trained novices. Being able to perform operations quickly is beneficial towards both the pa-tient and the surgeon.

It is observed that the implementation of virtual reality simulator training impacts operation time by significantly reducing the time required to com-plete the procedure. A simulator trained group compared with a control group performing live surgery over 21 separate operations suggests that surgeons learning through operating theaters complete their procedure in 12 minutes compared to the control group who completed their surgery in 24 minutes (Larsen et al., 2009). Furthermore, subjects performing laparoscopy training through virtual reality on the gallbladder with comparable baseline experi-ence to non-virtual reality trained subjects were observed to perform their dissections 29% faster (Seymour et al., 2002). As recognition and efficiency is enhanced through simulation based practice, dexterity and competence is also simultaneously improved to successfully and more accurately perform surgeries.

TECHNICAL SKILLS

The competence of a surgeon is described by a learning curve, which surgeons through clinical or virtual reality enhanced practice, developing their skills from novice to expert performance levels (Larsen et al., 2009). Competence is primarily assessed by the surgeon's technical skills and errors while com-pleting a successful surgery (Larsen et al., 2009). One of the surgical complications surrounding laparoscopic procedures is that they are fundamentally different and associated with much higher operation times compared to traditional open surgery; as a result, are associated with a more prolonged learning curve (Larsen et al., 2009). To be considered an expert laparoscopic surgeon, Denmark requires up to nine years of specialist training, two years of which are general and introductory training (Larsen et al., 2009). At the beginning of the specialist training, significant differences were observed among the subjects, as virtual reality trained surgeons were much more successful and showed higher levels of technical skill, with six times fewer errors; however, towards the end of their specialization, all subjects were achieving the same level of performance (Seymour et al., 2002). Virtual reality training among upcoming surgeons can effectively reduce the required training time to achieve expert competence; furthermore, new methods of surgery that are developed can be simulated to teach professional surgeons.

Patient safety is highly regarded when considering delicate and sensitive organs. The psycho-motor obstacles requiring precision is presented in laparoscopy and is transferable throughout all branches of surgical practice (Larsen et al., 2009). To perfect technical skills through training, a novice surgeon encounters the limiting resource of patients, often times requiring to shadow a supervisor before performing hands on practice without the intervention of a superior (Seymour et al., 2002). Due to the somewhat limiting technology supporting virtual reality, advanced skill acquisition is a difficult task; however, rudimentary technical skills that were often taught in operating rooms or were done in animal laboratories can allow surgeons to practice as many times as possible without creating ethical or health concerns (Seymour et al., 2002). Without a lack of resources to inhibit the growth of upcoming surgeons, virtual reality provides a means of learning to enhance technical skills and reduce errors which is beneficial for both parties, receiving and performing surgery.

CONCLUSION

The most important goal of any training method is to increase the level of skill transferred to the operating room, which virtual reality provides proficiency and technique early in the developing stages of introductory surgery, without creating inconveniences. The future of medicine is complicated and is very much dependent on current and developing technologies; however, computer simulations today allow for the implementation of new methods of teaching and approaching surgery. Newer developed surgical procedures such as minimally invasive surgeries which are not taught with conventional teaching methods, and persisting procedures are converged with the aid of virtual and augmented reality. Allowing for extensive practice in a wide array of fields without the presence of a patient, and with very little economical complications, it is a reasonable solution to the problems which forces the teaching of surgery to consider new approaches. The typical issues regarding medicine will continue to remain, thus as advanced technologies emerge, it is important to harness them and find solutions accordingly.

WORKS CITED

Seymour N. E., Gallagher A. G., Roman S. A., O'Brien M. K., Bansal V. K., Andersen D. K., Satava R. M. (2002) Virtual reality training improves operating room performance: Results of a randomized, double blind study. *Annals of Surgery* 236, 458–464. https://www.ncbi.nlm.nih.gov/pmc/articles/PMC1422600/

Larsen, C. R., Soerensen, J. L., Grantcharov, T. P., Dalsgaard, T., Schouenborg, L., Ottosen, C., Schroeder T. V. Ottesen B. S. (2009). Effect of virtual reality training on laparoscopic surgery: Randomised controlled trial. *Bmj* 338, 1253–1256. http://www.bmj.com/content/338/bmj.b1802

3.
EMERGING TECHNOLOGY
AND SOCIETY

A New Future for Language: The Internet

Kimberly Hsu

THE INTERNET IS a relatively new technological innovation that has continued to advance since its existence. It has certainly transformed many people's lives. But what impact will the Internet have on language? David Crystal addresses this question of 'Internet Linguistics' in his book, *Language and the Internet*, by suggesting that the "Internet has encouraged a dramatic expansion in the variety and creativity of language" (i). The Internet holds boundless possibilities for language and culture, which will enhance how one views the world as a truly diverse and global community. By allowing for the diversity of languages, the Internet decreases linguistic dominance and thus, it enriches every language and culture.

Crystal explores the interrelationship between language and the Internet through four main domains: email, chat groups, virtual worlds, and the Web. The common central idea, explained through these domains, is that the Internet has transformed how language is used (Crystal 5). As people connect and communicate with one another through these portals, there is an "...emergence of a distinctive variety of language..."(Crystal 258). Crystal investigates into 'Netspeak', which he defines as 'Internet Language'(19); for example, the use of "smileys" and how those convey one's facial expression over the Internet (39). Many of the ways of how people intercommunicate involve brief interactions that may be in the form of a text or a Facebook message, and might even contain abbreviations. Regarding this, Crystal suggests that "the arrival of new, informal, even bizarre forms of language extends the range of our sensitivity to linguistic contrasts" (275). The Internet is always being updated and new platforms are often emerging within it, which is why it "[enriches] the range of communicative options..." and contributes to 'linguistic diversity' (Crystal 276). Some might ponder whether 'Netspeak' will put other languages at risk, but as Crystal states, "there is no indication...of Netspeak replacing or threatening already existing varieties" (275). Rather than posing a threat, the Internet encourages variation which stimulates the development and enrichment of languages.

The Internet is a non-exclusive platform where one does not need permission nor special qualities to access it. In reality, not all can utilize it due to different circumstances, such as the struggling economies of Third World countries. However, "at least in principle, once their countries' infrastructure and internal economy allow them to gain access," it is simply "a medium in which the whole world participates" (Crystal 5). The Internet's universal nature promotes diversity and cross-cultural understanding. Since users from all over the globe use the Internet, there is a fascinating form of communication and connection that stretches to the many different parts of the world. Examples include one learning a foreign new language through an online program or learning about different countries and cultures through photos shared on social media. The ways in which one can explore and share different cultures are endless. Furthermore, many of the Internet's resources and much of its information are available in increasingly more languages. As Crystal describes it, "Not only does it offer a home to all linguistic styles within a language; it offers a home to all languages..." (229). This expands the Internet's 'multilinguistic inclusiveness' (Crystal 229) which further shapes and contributes to its growth as a global community.

The future, from a linguistic perspective, is optimistic. Technology is advancing rapidly and shifting a big part of people's lives onto the Internet. As this process takes place, "new technologies...will integrate the Internet with other communication situations, and these will provide the matrix within which further language varieties will develop" (Crystal 258). Perhaps, as Crystal describes it, people "are on the brink of the biggest language revolution ever" (275).

As explained, the Internet is an incredibly diverse platform that fosters multiculturalism and multilingualism. Due to its global nature and way of operating, the Internet decreases linguistic dominance, also known as global language dominance, and provides new ways to resolve the disadvantages of it. As people are free to share their languages and cultures online, diversity is spread. In this way, people have a better understanding and more access to the global community. Therefore, the drawbacks of linguistic dominance, such as exclusion, superiority, and more, are resolved. Also, speakers of minority languages can freely promote their languages on the Internet, which can save those endangered languages from disappearing. The Internet enables each and every language to be equally precious. Furthermore, it aids and allows for variations and diversity within a language itself. Thus, the Internet is a gateway, enriching language and culture, that grants one access to more of the world.

WORKS CITED

Crystal, David. *Language and the Internet.* 2nd ed., Cambridge University Press, 2006.

How Can VR Be Used to Improve the Reactions of Ice Hockey Goalies?

Aric Wolstenholme

LITTLE RESEARCH HAS been done on the application of virtual reality (VR) for training ice hockey goaltenders' reactions to shots. Currently, there is a knowledge deficit of how ice hockey goaltenders react to high-speed shots. Most research towards ice hockey goalies is focused on physical training and conditioning, and the mental side of the game. Meanwhile, reaction speed research focuses on ball sports, such as cricket in Peter McLeod`s "visual reaction time and high-speed ball games". Similarly, most VR research towards sports is done on ball sports, such as baseball, tennis, and handball, not hockey. It is possible that current virtual reality technology and research could be applied as a training tool for ice hockey goaltenders.

An ice hockey goalie is required to quickly react to the shooter, puck, and players around him or her to save the puck. Goaltenders are relied upon to save shots of speeds up to 175.1 kilometers per hour from multiple angles and distances. During games, goalies must make split-second decisions as to how they will react to the shot. They need to read the angle of the shooter's blade upon release, their eyes, and the rise and trajectory of the puck. While the goalie is reading these signals, they must decide the best method to save the puck. If it is not possible to trap the puck, they must decide where to send the rebound depending on the position of opposing players around them. Then, if the rebound goes to an opposing player, they need to reposition and perform the series of reactions again, with even less time than before. In order to succeed, goalies in ice hockey must have exceptional reaction speeds and anticipation.

Peter McLeod's "Visual reaction time and high-speed ball games" focuses on the differences in reactions between amateur and professional cricket players. McLeod performed two experiments to measure the reactions of professional cricket players compared to amateur players. The first experiment measured the amount of time required for the batsmen to react to a ball's change in direction. A bowling machine launched a ball which would contact an uneven surface before a batsman would attempt to hit the ball. Data was also collected from footage of professional international games. McLeod found that both amateur players and professional players react "in a narrow temporal band between 190 and 240 ms" (McLeod, 1987). On average, both groups of players required 200 milliseconds to perceive a change in the ball's motion and thus change their positioning. No player reacted "in less than 190 ms after [a change in direction]" (McLeod, 1987). Although both groups of players reacted to a change in direction within the same interval, the professional players made contact with the ball more often. Since both amateur and professional players' time to react are similar, McLeod concluded another factor must determine the success of professionals.

McLeod's second experiment discovered the reason for the professional players' success. He played videos of a bowler pitching balls towards a camera placed where a batsman would stand. The tapes would stop at different times, right before the ball leaves the bowler's hand, "or 80,160, or 240 ms later" (McLeod, 1987). People watching the tapes would have to predict whether the pitch was short, good length, or overpitched. Results showed the professional players possessed "profoundly impressive visual-motor skills" (McLeod, 1987). They were about 6% better than the amateur players at predicting overpitched and good length pitches. Therefore, it is a professional ability to predict where they should swing, not their reaction speed which separates them from amateurs.

Cricket batsmen and ice hockey goaltenders experience similar situations. Both batsmen and ice hockey goalies encounter balls or pucks moving towards them at high speeds. Batsmen interpret whether a pitch is short, good length or overpitched and whether it is moving to the left, center or right. Similarly, a goaltender deciphers whether a shot is high, medium or low and whether it is to the left, center or right. The ball in cricket can bounce in random directions, like how a puck can be deflected by other players in a hockey game. In order to succeed in their sport, reaction speeds and anticipation of both types of players need to be excellent.

Due to their similarities, the findings of McLeod's experiment can be applied to ice hockey goaltenders. If a cricket player's average reaction time was 200 milliseconds for both professionals and amateurs, it is most likely the same for ice hockey goalies. This is because both amateur and professional cricket players had about the same reaction time. Therefore, it must be the average reaction time for humans, which has a maximum of about 190 milliseconds. Consequently, amateur and professional ice hockey goalies most likely have the same reaction time of around 200 milliseconds. The main difference between professional and amateur cricket players was their ability to predict the location of the ball. As a result, to improve a goaltender's reactions to shots, their anticipation of shots needs to be trained the most. There was a 6% difference between amateur and professional cricketers in their ability to predict the ball's final location. In professional ice hockey, a 6% difference in save percentage is substantial; it is the difference between an elite starting goalie and a minor- league goalie. If virtual reality is to be used to train goaltenders reactions, it should improve their ability to predict where the puck will travel.

"A review of virtual environments for training in ball sports" by Helen C. Miles, Serban R. Pop, Simon J. Watt, Gavin P. Lawrence, and Nigel W. John describes how to successfully utilize virtual reality for sports training. Four key standards must be followed for virtual reality to successfully train athletes in sports. First, the movements performed in virtual reality should be the same as in real life. Second, there must be a variety of variables for each simulation so it is not the same each time. Third, during each simulation, the person in the simulation should know outcomes of their performed actions. Finally, the different outcomes should all administer sensory effects to the person in the simulation. If any of these criteria are not met "the [virtual environment] does not adequately approximate the information in the real-world setting" and it is not useful for training (Miles, 2012).

Helen C. Miles et al. describes a successful handball goalkeeper simulation which effectively trains goalkeepers. A handball goaltender wearing a head-mounted display (HMD) to view a stereoscopic virtual environment, stands in front of the net with coloured tiles in each corner, while a camera captures the goalie's movements. The goaltender is presented with a virtual opponent who he must stop from scoring a goal. When the goaltender moves to stop the virtual ball the camera captures his movement and applies it to the HMD. Originally the system was used to study the difference in reaction to virtual opponent compared to real ones. However, Miles' study revealed that the system "[provoked] real defensive movement from the goalkeeper" and it could be a reliable training tool (Miles, 2012). Simulations of the virtual opponent could be changed in a variety of ways to train goaltenders in many situations and specific skills. It is also relatively cheap and easy to use the system while following all four of the criteria for a successful training tool. The simulation is effective enough that Germany uses it to train its youth handball goalkeepers.

Ice hockey could apply the handball simulation to improve a goaltender's anticipation of shots. Instead of taking place on a hardwood floor in front of a handball net, the set-up would be transferred to an ice surface in front of a hockey net. The ice hockey goaltender would wear all of the same gear, except the helmet, which would be replaced by the HMD. Coloured tiles would be placed in each corner and a camera to capture the goaltender's movements would be placed in front of him or her. The simulation would have to be re-programmed so the virtual opponent is an ice hockey player, not a handball player. The virtual opponent can be programmed to take shots aimed at different areas of the net from varying locations at high speeds. This allows the goaltender to practice anticipating shots by reading the stick angle and body of the opponent for different shots. If the goaltender has trouble in certain situations, the simulation can focus just on those. Since it is a virtual reality simulation, if taught how to use it, a goaltender can train on their own and not rely on a capable shooter. If they have synthetic ice installed in their home, or have access to an ice surface, they can train whenever they want. Through the simulation, any level goaltender can improve their reactions to shots and increase their save percentage.

Current virtual reality technology can be combined with research on the reaction in sports to improve ice hockey goaltenders' reactions. Peter Mc-Leod's "Visual reaction time and high-speed ball games" reveals how it is the anticipation of the location of a cricket ball which differentiates professionals from amateurs. "A review of virtual environments for training in ball sports" by Helen C. Miles et al. describes a virtual reality simulation which is used to train handball goalkeepers. Both concepts can be applied to ice hockey as virtual reality system to improve the anticipation of ice hockey goaltenders to train their reactions. If such a system were created, the effects could be studied to erase the current knowledge deficit.

WORKS CITED

McLeod, Peter. "Visual reaction time and high-speed ball games." *Perception* 16.1 (1987): 49–59.

Miles, Helen C., et al. "A review of virtual environments for training in ball sports." *Computers & Graphics* 36.6 (2012): 714–726.

Developing Virtual Reality Fights Against Gender Inequality In the Video Game Industry

Anna (Zhouyu) Yan

IN THE CONTEMPORARY video game field, much of the related content seems to be dominated by men, such that related industries are mostly considered to target male consumers. Take virtual reality as an example, "the industry's biggest investments are being made in adrenaline-fuelled gaming experiences and pornography" as reported in the showcase hosted Virtual Reality LA. Because males market seems to make up the target audience of video game industry, females have few opportunities to voice themselves through their storytelling and create female genre programmes in video games. Virtual reality may still be an infant realm in platforms of the video game industry, but it is widely considered to hold the most potential relative to similar technological areas. Can virtual reality change the unequal situation in video game industry and offer an opportunity for females to create an even playing field?

Women figures are found to be objectified and disrespected in the general video games. Female characters are more likely than male characters to be portrayed as in a sexual manner (60% versus 1%). The severe effect of stereotypical or sexualized female figure in the technology is underestimated. Such negative images are so powerful, which impacts both gamer and non-gamers, extending their negative influences into real-life. A study performed by Jesse Fox suggested that the sexualized characters in a video game can have adverse mental effects. They designed to invite 86 women from West Coast university played a virtual reality game in the study. Women who used sexualized characters that looked like them were found to have a higher rape myth acceptance than those in other situation. The researchers think it to be the "validation of incorrect and stereotypical ideas about rape that blame the victim", and "increased body-related thinking which can lead to increased self-objectification". It suggests to higher the possibility of developing harsh attitudes to other women and their own selves in reality by using sexualized characters in technology such as video games. On the other hand, Karen E. Dill and Kathryn P. Thill place an experiment on the boys who play video games. They found out that they are ignorant of the adverse impacts of detestable media content, and therefore ignorant of that when they are affected adversely. The study illustrates the ways prominent video game characters are gendered and what is received by the user or viewer. They found that the gender portrayals of video game characters reinforce "a sexist, patriarchal view that men are aggressive and powerful" and that "women are not healthy, whole persons, but sex objects, eye candy and generally second-class citizens." The information conveyed through media like video games is subtly changing the mindset of the society.

However, how can women stand up and speak out for themselves when games and stories featuring women are almost entirely absent and the figure of women are totally distorted in this rapidly growing technology industry?

Under such circumstances, some virtual reality producers see where the original video game companies went wrong and are utilizing virtual reality as a new platform to create female related programs. Catherine Allen, a female virtual reality programmer, promotes virtual reality game that is a talk show targeting millennial women, filming two women talking in a coffee shop about topics that range from how to reduce anxiety, to their opinions on the current political situation. Some opinions are saying that this program not only presents how young women see the world but also offers a rational and non-stereotypical picture of women to the public. The complex topics discussed on the show reveals the complexity of women, displaying a more accurate image of women as actual humans. It contrasts the sexy fighting machines without intelligence that is often portrayed in video games. Virtual reality programs like the talk show are highly accessible to women and are starting to be embraced by all different groups as well.

Virtual reality allows participants to step into a different body and become the protagonist in the program. This key aspect of virtual reality allows it to be used in such way that it enables the users to experience some of the tragic inequalities that women face. This potential of virtual reality to create such vivid experiences is being explored by a female filmmaker, Jayisha Patel. For example, in the documentary Note to My Father that explores the story of an Indian human-trafficking survivor, one of the most harrowing scenes positions the viewer inside "a train carriage full of men". It aims to depict a vivid perspective that is the subject of the male gaze. "Through the headset, the viewers can truly feel being 'objectified' by being the only woman in the carriage and having all these men staring at you, hearing them adjust their belts, breathing heavily." With the potential that virtual reality has as a tool for creating empathy, Jayisha Patel, the film developer, managed to find the way to use virtual reality to convey an important message about what life is like for women. With any luck, virtual reality will be able to help to break down the barriers between genders by positioning people to get better at seeing points of view of others.

Additionally, the developing virtual reality industry is in its infancy stage, women have a chance to get in at the ground level and reflect their talents. Compared to the gender disparity in the workplace in the traditional video game field, virtual reality offers more positions for women. The latest figures from games industry trade body, TIGA, show that "only 14% of people working in the UK games industry are women" In contrast, in a survey conducted in January 2017, among 70 out of hundreds of international virtual reality companies, around 64.3% of the participants said that their company were led by women founders. Women in virtual reality workplace are breaking the barriers in the video game industry.

On the other hand, an unfortunate gender difference issue presented by virtual reality technology is that women have shown to be generally more prone to motion sickness than men when using the virtual reality equipment. A group of researchers from the University of Minnesota, who have been studying motion sickness for over 15 years, suggest that women are indeed more likely to suffer from motion sickness— such as traditional seasickness and carsickness—but that this situation happens to women more obviously and often when using virtual reality devices like the Oculus Rift. The experiment followed body movement of the participants when playing a Rift game for 15 minutes, following which researchers then recorded the number of people who felt nauseous. The result showed that the incidence of motion sickness was 38% among women, but only 9% among men. The study also claims that motion sickness induced using in virtual reality exhibited sex differences greater than those that have been reported in field studies. Due to the fact that 80 percent of the subjects who felt unwell within ten minutes were women, some arguments are saying that it is a major design flaw in the virtual reality equipment such as Oculus Rift. The crew believes that people who have higher centres of gravity, larger feet and are heavier, are more likely to stabilise their bodies. It just so happens that men are considered to be taller and heavier, and have larger feet than women.

But it doesn't mean that virtual reality has no way of solving this gender bias in the motion sickness in virtual reality experience. Danah Boyd, from

Microsoft, spotted the motion sickness problem to women in her virtual reality game programming. She started a research to find the difference in how men and women experience the various methods VR producers use to suggest distance, "Motion parallax, which uses perspective to suggest distance, is processed far better by men than women; shape-from-shading, which uses light to alter the way you perceive objects, is processed better by women." Most virtual reality systems use motion parallax because it is easier to program and cost less than shape-from-shading. When motion parallax, however, makes the virtual reality experience far less pleasurable for women, the designers are supposed to improve the system to create enjoyable virtual reality experience for female. The motion sickness issue is thought to be the biggest obstacle that developers should come across in the process of fighting against gender inequality in the video game industry.

Until now, even though the design of virtual reality needs improvement to equally give all the people an opportunity of pleasuring experience, virtual reality is doing something that cannot be done in other platforms to fight against the gender inequality in video games. A number of virtual reality producers are determined to prevent virtual reality from sharing the same fate as other entertainment platforms and tech sectors, as well as from becoming a male-dominated experience. Virtual reality is standing by for women to reclaim the gender gap in technological development by making content for and about women.

WORKS CITED

Boyd, Danah. *Depth Cues in Virtual Reality and Real World: Understanding Individual Differences in Depth Perception by Studying Shape-from-Shading and Motion Parallax.* Publisher: Brown University (2005). DOI: /10.1371/journal. pone.0003177

Chakareski, Jacob. "VR/AR Immersive Communication." *Proceedings of the Workshop on Virtual Reality and Augmented Reality Network—VR/AR Network 17*, 2017, doi:10.1145/3097895.3097902.

Dill, K.E. & Thill, K.P. *Video Game Characters and the Socialization of Gender Roles: Young People's Perceptions Mirror Sexist Media Depictions* (2007) 57: 851. DOI:10.1007/s11199-007-9278-1

Fox, J., Bailenson, J. N., & Tricase, L. (2013). The embodiment of sexualized virtual selves: The Proteus effect and experiences of self-objectification via avatars. *Computers in Human Behavior*, 29(3), 930–938. DOI: 10.1016/j.chb.2012.12.027

Koslucher, Frank; Haaland, Eric; Malsch, Amy; Webeler, Jennifer; Stoffregen, Thomas A. Sex Differences in the Incidence of Motion Sickness Induced by Linear Visual Oscillation. *Aerospace Medicine and Human Performance*, Volume 86, Number 9, September 2015, pp. 787–793(7). Publisher: Aerospace Medical Association. DOI:10.3357/AMHP.4243.2015

Lemons, M.A. & Parzinger, M. J. Gender Schemas: A Cognitive Explanation of Discrimination of Women in Technology. *Bus Psycho* (2007) 22: 91. DOI: 10.1007/s10869-007-9050-0

Patel, J. (2017, February 2). Note to my Father. Retrieved November 27, 2017, from British Council